THE VOLUNTEER SHELF LIFE

A No Fault Look at Volunteer Retention and the Reasons Volunteers Leave

D0872418

MERIDIAN SWIFT

ISBN: 1463766971
ISBN-13: 9781463766979

Chapter 1

Can We Retain Volunteers Forever?

Managing volunteers is challenging. No, really.

Are volunteers similar to employees, or are they so dissimilar that we should not even compare the two? How do those of us that work with volunteers recruit, place, and retain them on a daily basis while maintaining a healthy balance between the HR model and the heart of volunteering? This area of human resources is tricky. Results are expected while the well-being of the volunteers—which includes their motivations, expectations, satisfaction, and return quotient—rests on the shoulders of the volunteer manager. One of the primary issues of volunteer management is retention. How do we get our volunteers to stay with us? Once a person inquires about volunteering, it is our duty to attract, train, prepare, and keep that volunteer, or so the perception goes. But volunteers are no different from employees in that they, too, have varied motivations and reasons to work with us. And, taking that one step further, their reasons to leave are even more wide-ranging than the reasons they came to us in the first place. Because volunteers are not bound to us financially, their decision to leave can be made in an instant. Is that our fault, and must we cling to the notion that once we snag a volunteer, it is our obligation to keep him/her indefinitely, no matter the circumstance? In our changing world, volunteers will be more likely to stay with us for short periods of time. It is time to stop blaming ourselves when a volunteer leaves.

This Is Too Difficult

Carmen was a volunteer manager at an organization that provided meals to seniors who were homebound. The area covered was rural and wide, but Carmen enthusiastically took on her job as volunteer coordinator, knowing that the importance of serving lonely seniors would be enough to attract good helpers. This organization offered mileage reimbursement as an incentive to travel the country roads. Sometimes, homes were tucked away in the woods, or at the end of a bumpy gravel driveway. Carmen set about recruiting through newspaper ads, flyers, and speaking engagements where she made passionate pleas for help. She ended up attracting twenty newcomers in her first orientation. After the initial training, the volunteers, fresh with zeal for the work, would take two and three clients. Then, like clockwork, they would deliver the meals for a few weeks and the calls would begin. Carmen would pick up her messages to hear, "I'm having car trouble," or, "I'm not feeling well." Carmen would then drive the routes to deliver the meals herself. She would continue her search to replace missing volunteers while doing their work. She offered abbreviated training, and the chance to drive once a month instead of every week. Still, her numbers remained low, and she found that the majority of her time was spent on the road, out of the office and away from recruiting. In frustration, Carmen quit and went to work at a local bookstore.

No Man Is an Island

Sam, a longtime volunteer manager at a large metropolitan museum, was attending a national conference on volunteer management. He was sitting in a session that focused on recruiting teen volunteers. Having worked for many years with local teens, Sam thought he would learn some tips for engaging them. Sam said, "You know the type of presentations that feature a slick PowerPoint show about an innovative program with an enviable retention rate." The presenters were terminally cheery and threw out teaser facts about their program. To hear the history, Sam thought the presenters had discovered the panacea of volunteer management. He recalled that there was not one pitfall presented, not one problem, not one story of a teen that didn't work out. He said it was around the time the presenters claimed that the "teen volunteers will love this program so much that they will be the best volunteers you've ever had," that he got up and walked out. He didn't admire the presenters for their well-crafted message. He didn't write down the e-mail address to later purchase their packaged program highlights. He said he walked out of the room, leaned against the wall and started to laugh. He couldn't help it; he found in that moment, in that presentation, the disconnect that had been gnawing at him for some time. He wondered if he was the only volunteer manager who was realistic when it came to the challenges of managing vast numbers of unpaid workers. He wondered if the others in the room were navigating the joys and pitfalls of volunteer management. At that moment, he felt more alone than at any other time in his long, successful career. He wondered if he was completely burned out or if he just craved honesty.

Managing volunteers is a noble profession, a wonderful job, but all too often, the very peers that we feel will understand our situations offer positive volunteer stories and ignore any problems so as to place an encouraging spin on things. Why is that, do you think? Why are we not honest about the realities of volunteers and the complex issues of managing them? It is human nature not to wish to air problems or shortcomings. We like to shed a positive light on our volunteer programs, perhaps because we are eternally optimistic or because we want to help each other. But what often happens is we give the incorrect impression that by managing volunteers a certain way, all problems will disappear. This is not true. We place so much emphasis on volunteer retention that we falsely begin to believe that retention is the goal of volunteer management, instead of providing the best service for our clients.

Different Does Not Mean Equal

Think about the different ways in which we view employees versus volunteers. We even use differing language for each group, which is a disparity that will give you some indication as to how these two groups are perceived. When employees retire, we throw them a retirement party complete with envious guests. We slap them on the back, recap all the wonderful things they've done for the organization, and send them out in a blaze of gold watch glory. We rib them, muse on how nice it will be when we get to that stage, and how we'll be able to do whatever it is we want. Ahhh. Contrast that with a volunteer retiring. I don't mean a volunteer who cannot do the job any longer due to illness or infirmity. I mean the volunteers who decide to stop. Do we fete them? Do we envy them? Do we say, "Hey, you've made it!" No, we cringe, look inward, and wonder what we did to make them "quit." Do you ever see a company wonder why an employee retired? Do companies try and keep employees until they are elderly and frail and can't do the job anymore?

Let's take this one step further. If an employee quits, does the company beat itself up endlessly? Yes, companies spend a great deal of time and energy trying to retain really good employees, and therein lies the similarity, as we all try to retain the very best people for our needs. But unlike companies, who use the opportunity to work on retention as a process, most volunteer managers take the exodus of a volunteer personally. Volunteer managers beat themselves up when a volunteer chooses to leave. What did I do wrong? What did I miss? What should I have done better? We mire ourselves in blame, never looking at the system or forces beyond our control. We should have run interference when staff failed to call the volunteer the day they didn't need her, or we should have known instinctively that the volunteer's spouse was ill, even though he never said a word to us. We should have seen that breakdown coming or that change in life circumstance. Truth be told, we are a bit masochistic when it comes to volunteer retention. Any volunteer, even a poor or mediocre one, who leaves is a blot on our record. We automatically consider it a failure when a volunteer leaves, no matter what the reason. It is as if volunteering has a magical draw that outweighs circumstance, change, and personality. If we are painfully honest, don't we feel a twinge of guilt even when a poor volunteer leaves? Somehow, like the clingy friend, we feel that we should have been the ones to straighten that person out; that the sheer wonderfulness of the work we do and offer will turn even the worst person into a productive volunteer. And when that does not happen, all eyes settle on us, because we did not do our job. After all, isn't it all about recruitment and retention? Aren't sheer numbers indicative of happy, perfect, unpaid helpers? This is one of the myths of volunteer management. Every person who inquires about volunteering does so out of the goodness of his/her heart. And every person who inquires about volunteering will turn out to be a wonderful, award-winning example of perfect volunteerism. And if those perfect volunteers leave, then it must be the fault of the volunteer manager.

So what fuels this notion? It could be because our organizations have a long history of really good volunteers making a tremendous difference in the lives of the people we serve. This says a lot about the people who have stepped forward to volunteer over the years. Not all, but the vast majority of people who volunteer do so out of the goodness of their hearts and add a rich layer to each organization's mission. In many instances, organizations could not survive without all the help afforded by volunteers.

However, volunteer managers are excellent at recruiting, screening, training, and mentoring volunteers. We have to be exceptional at it. We do not have a paycheck to dangle over anyone's head. Therefore, we work extra hard at making sure the right person fits into the right position. We check, we double-check, and then we follow up. We talk to the volunteer, we talk to the people working with the volunteer, and we talk with the recipient of the help. Can you imagine doing that with staff? There is no time to do that with staff, but somehow we make it happen with volunteers. With staff, you give them an assignment and the responsibility to complete that assignment rests with the staff member. With volunteers, in many ways the responsibility to complete a given assignment rests with the volunteer manager. We take good people and complete all the groundwork to help them succeed.

But if you think about it, we derail a great many problems that crop up. We keep problems from happening. We dance around enough to know who can waltz, who can jitterbug, and who will trip every time. That clumsy person is relegated to office work, or special functions, or whatever we can ease him/her into doing. We have to be honest, though. We don't let management know about problems too often. We pretty much paint a very rosy picture, one that has become ingrained into the psyche of our respective organizations and the general public. We are not very good at airing the pitfalls, the zaniness, or the crazy situations we deal with week after week.

In short, we can shoot ourselves in the foot by making everything "look easy." How many times do volunteer managers lament that no one really knows what we do? This is probably the most common complaint I've heard from those who work with volunteers every day. Part of our reluctance to paint anything but a perfect picture is that we are protective of our volunteers. Notice how I use the possessive "our"? We tend to become personally responsible for the actions of the volunteers in our charge and we are extremely protective of them. We don't want staff and administration thinking ill of them. We want them to get the respect they deserve. Most volunteer managers would rather go down themselves than allow someone in their organization to disparage one of the volunteers, even if that volunteer might deserve it.

So, what to do? Do we air all our dirty laundry, share all our problems, and run the risk of having the organization look at all volunteers as potential lawsuits waiting to happen? Do we destroy our own careers when administration decides to do away with volunteers altogether? Or do we continue to make everything look easy, make staff members believe that we just chat all day with sweet little ladies and then plan tea parties?

There must be a happy medium. If we can show the tremendous benefits that volunteers bring to our organizations, surely there will be a bit of wiggle room when we also let them know that not all volunteers are alike, and they, just like their paid counterparts, are human, with ups and downs, varied reasons to be with us, and a period of time that they will serve, whether by their choice or ours. We must educate our organizations that volunteers have a shelf life, that volunteers belong to the organization and not to us personally, and that we are really human resource managers extraordinaire. Simply put, there must be a balance. As we are too reluctant to discuss the realities of this vast unpaid staffing pool, we are also sometimes ill-equipped to show the many benefits volunteers bring. Money saved is the most common measure of a volunteer program. Actually, volunteers don't save money at all. If you think about it, your organization would most likely not hire staff to do what your volunteers do. So, volunteers don't save money, they enhance services. They make the lives of those we help so much better. If you can find ways to measure that, by all means do so. It may take some really long and hard thinking to be able to measure these outcomes, but it is worth it. If your volunteers provide respite to a patient's family, that is measurable. If your volunteers provide tutoring for disadvantaged children, that is measurable. Statistics such as 80 percent of all seniors that needed a ride to the hospital to receive treatment were able to keep their appointments due to volunteer involvement is an impressive number. But don't stop there. Anecdotal examples bring the numbers into perspective, so pepper your statistics with some inspiring stories. If you are not sure exactly what impact the volunteers have on a client, ask him/her. Find out what the benefit of having volunteer help is and then account for it. By asking, you may find that volunteers are helping in more ways than you originally thought. For instance, in hospice, we polled the family members who benefited from having a volunteer sit with their loved one while they went out. Not only did they benefit in the traditional way, they told us about secondary benefits, such as the volunteer provided socialization and helped the patient to relax, which made for a good night's sleep. From those interviews, we found many more benefits that we could point to in a report.

Remind your organization that by accepting volunteers, it is showing the community that it is an open and transparent entity. By having volunteers who are a slice of the general public, the organization has agreed to be scrutinized by members of the surrounding area. Volunteers also spread the word about the great job the organization is doing. They recruit other volunteers and potential clients for your organization. If there is a way to measure how many new clients came because a volunteer recommended them, then by all means record that. Volunteers can also become staff members, as many eventually want to work for the organization. These volunteers turned staff are usually those we already know well and, conversely, they know us too, so they make smart additions to our workforce. Part of the reason they end up applying for a job in our organization is because they had a good introduction via their volunteer training and experience. Take some credit for that. Is it fair to say that volunteers offer our organizations that extra human touch, but at the same time, managing them can be challenging, and yet the rewards for our clients far outweigh any challenges?

The perpetuated notion that volunteers are really all the same, have nothing better to do and will never cause problems, much less have opinions, may keep the volunteers themselves looking very good in the eyes of staff and community, but this notion makes volunteer managers look bad, because how hard is it to keep such angelic people? Are we sometimes not our own worst enemy when it involves the reality of managing volunteers? We tend to keep to ourselves the stories about the volunteer who calls us three times a day, asking for an assignment because she needs one, or the prospective volunteer who shows up at our desk to announce that a divine voice told him to come there. It may be difficult to recount some of the crazier stories to those who do not work in our profession, but we should be able to share with each other. After all, we do understand what each one of us is going through. I once asked another volunteer manager if she had any stories of difficult or funny volunteers. She looked at me blankly and said no. After telling her a few stories of my own, she opened up and in a conspiratorial tone told me about a few incidents that were just as crazy.

When we realize that there are circumstances beyond our control and there are limits to a volunteer's stay with us, we can stop beating ourselves up for the ones that "get away." Instead, we can focus on the volunteers we have while we have them, and be proud of the hard work we do with them. Recruiting volunteers is like panning for gold. There are going to be those that just wash through the pan. We may have to filter through several people to find that one gold nugget. Volunteering is not for everyone. Not everyone has the temperament to take instruction on how to help others. Not everyone sees the benefit. Not everyone can focus on the big picture or on the person he/she is supposed to help. So, as you pan for the gold, and you watch the other pieces fall through and back into the river, don't let guilt wash over you because you could not mold that person into another perfect gold nugget. Take pride in the fact that you have a discerning eye, that you are careful enough to find the gold, and that you don't take just any piece of rock and paint it gold so that you can inflate your numbers. The message should be that we, as volunteer managers, are picky so that those who help our vulnerable charges are the very best. Never would we offer an unqualified person who might potentially do harm.

As the baby boomers replace the WWII generation, we are faced with new volunteer challenges. You may find that you have to have three part-time volunteers for every one job. Boomers are less interested in routine, less interested in jobs that do not challenge them, less interested in jobs they perceive as meaningless, and are not interested at all in jobs that do not contribute to their vision of self. As we attempt to recruit them by changing verbiage (boomers would rather hear *mentor* than *helper*), and restructure volunteer opportunities to reflect a higher level of input (create leader roles), we have to be prepared for volunteer commitment to change. One report on boomers floated the idea that we stop using the word *volunteer*. Again, the notion that we must bend over backward to make everything perfect for volunteers can only set us up for personal failure. Certainly, we should make volunteering for our organizations as attractive as possible. And as the complexion of volunteering changes, we must change with it. It is the implied message of failure if, after implementing innovation and change, we still lose volunteers that is wrong. We will lose some no matter what we do. If we bend to every prospective volunteer's time line, wishes, and needs, then we will end up exhausted and spent. We will also end up with volunteers who are demanding and with us for the wrong reasons. Those volunteers will not last, even if we continue to feed their demands, because it will never be enough. The work is enough. The pride in truly helping others is enough. The joy of real gratitude from those we serve is enough. Instead of rearranging our trainings to fit anyone who calls and says, "Oh, do I have to wait a month? I wanted to start tomorrow," we should be fostering the idea that volunteering for our organizations is a privilege. We are worth the wait, worth the rules, worth starting at the bottom of the volunteer ladder. Use volunteer testimonial after testimonial. The message becomes, "This is a place where only the cream of the crop is accepted." Reject potential volunteers regularly and without apology. If the client were a relative of yours, how many of your volunteers would you be comfortable with helping your loved one? How many of the prospective volunteers you speak to would you be pleased to have helping your loved one? We can take pride in our stringent standards, and we can tell those who question why we don't have more volunteers that we will only provide the very best for our clients. Numbers are not our goal; quality is our goal. And as we strive to get the most qualified volunteers, it will also mean that we are rejecting more prospective people. How many hours are spent with volunteers that we accepted against our better judgment? We spend enormous amounts of time counseling them, mopping up their missteps, and shuffling them from job to job. While people deserve a chance, volunteer managers tend to give more chances than is prudent.

Are volunteer managers inherently nonconfrontational? Are we inherently meek, gentle souls that just want everyone to flourish? Although a nice concept on paper, it really isn't a practical way to manage people. Volunteers want and need direction. They respect clearly defined roles, rules, expectations, and feedback. The inability to tell a volunteer that he/she is wrong only prolongs the inevitable, so do not be apologetic for doing your job. All deserve the chance to get it right, and when we allow volunteers to get away with poor behavior, we do them a disservice. After all, we are not volunteer enablers, or volunteer doormats, or volunteer magicians—we are volunteer managers. Volunteers who take our orientations, strap on the badge, agree to the rules, and embrace the mission are the tools to enhance our clients' experiences. But tools wear out, get misplaced, and sometimes break. Volunteers, too, have a term of use. If we look at them in this way, see them for the temporary help they are, then we will stop berating ourselves when they are gone. Their time with us is precious, but not permanent. This is their shelf life.

Chapter 2

Are You Leaving Already?

Gone and Missed

A hospice volunteer manager I know wistfully spoke about her volunteer, Gregg, who seemed to have miraculously fallen from the sky. A younger gentleman, he was recently widowed when he approached her hospice to give back for the beautiful care his beloved wife of thirty-five years had received. After completing the bereavement sessions, he came to volunteer services with the gusto of a man on a mission. His mission was clear to him: extend the compassion and support to others experiencing the trauma that he had suffered. He felt there was no better way to memorialize his wife than by helping other men deal with the death of their soul mate and partner. Gregg breezed through orientation, accepted an assignment with a volunteer mentor, and cheerfully began his hospice career. This manager had high hopes for him, and after a good start, she gave Gregg his first assignment. Soon, Gregg had three and four patients; then, he started mentoring new volunteers and even took a few speaking engagements, in which he passionately described his meaningful experiences with patients. He became the go-to guy, especially since male volunteers were rare. Gregg had the ability to manage stressful situations with kindness and tact, as he brought his retired military sensibilities combined with a genuine desire to succeed. Gregg enjoyed learning new jobs and immersed himself in a leadership role, helping to manage the few males who volunteered.

I can see you sitting there, waiting for the hammer to fall. What happened? Did Gregg go off the deep end and steal from his patients? Was he not what he appeared? Or could he still be deeply grieving?

No, it was nothing so dramatic. After two years of exemplary service, Gregg came into the volunteer manager's office one afternoon and asked to talk. She had never seen him in such a giddy, nervous mood before, so they found a quiet place to talk. Gregg pulled out a picture of a lovely woman named Marcia, whom he had met six months before. They had started dating and now had decided to get married. Gregg was ecstatic.

Gregg was now going to start living a brand-new life, a life that did not include hospice work. Although he would miss the patients, the other volunteers, and most certainly the volunteer manager, Gregg was preparing to travel, to go to dinner, to reinvest in living. His time with hospice was over, not because he did not like the work anymore, and not because he stopped finding the patients interesting, but because he no longer needed it. He had closed that chapter. His immersion in volunteering did not have a prominent place in his new life. No longer did he need to help others the way he had been helped. This volunteer's shelf life lasted for as long as the work fulfilled his need. He had strengthened himself through helping other families. He had used his time for healing. Oftentimes, we chastise volunteers for using their patients or clients to mend their sorrows, but there are some volunteers who can walk that fine line and help not only everyone they come in contact with, but themselves as well.

At this point, when a volunteer has naturally completed his/her term of service, we can mourn our loss, or we can be grateful for the dual purpose we have served. Seeing volunteers get that much out of their work should be extremely satisfying. Bereavement has an ending by design, and sometimes we are part of that process. If the volunteers sincerely help others and heal their hearts, then we must be able to let them go. It's difficult to be happy when great volunteers leave because their life has taken a positive turn, because we are mentally tallying the hours of hard work it will take to replace them. We can bemoan the fact that they are abandoning us, or we can move on and be happy for them and proud of ourselves and our programs. It is another layer of volunteer services.

It is very difficult trying to explain to someone not in our field why a good volunteer, one who does great things, has chosen to leave. It is hard to explain that the volunteer has come to a natural, positive ending, because he/she has reached the point where we are the ones who are no longer needed.

Gone Too Soon

Julie was a vibrant, bubbly volunteer who filled any room with warmth and fun. A former flight attendant, now newly retired, Julie was living a life full of meaning and purpose. She gave to her church, her neighbors, and her community. She felt that she needed to do the most intimate and profound volunteer work she could imagine, so she chose a local nursing home that specialized in dementia patients. After her orientation, she was assigned to the dementia ward, where she cared for all of her patients as though they were her mother or father. She became fast friends and a favorite of the volunteer manager, who was genuinely happy to see Julie each time she breezed into the office. They would have lunch together on occasion, the volunteer manager picking Julie's brain to better understand motivations that might help in recruiting others like her. Wondering if Julie was an anomaly or indicative of a vast untapped resource, the manager used her for speaking engagements whenever she could. Julie exemplified the persons who volunteer purely to give back because they feel they are so fortunate or so blessed. These volunteers have a deep sense of commitment and payback, and can be counted on to need little from their volunteering except the knowledge that what they do truly makes a difference.

One day, however, Julie came into the office and was tense and weepy. Because she had such a strong relationship with the volunteer manager, she was able to reveal that her husband of thirty years was leaving her for another woman. He had already moved out. Julie was understandably devastated. No one who knew Julie could understand how her husband could have left her. With great sadness, she said she needed to take some time off, to figure out what she was going to do. Julie stepped back from her volunteer work. She kept in touch with her volunteer manager as a friend, but nothing more. She began to do other things, things that were vastly different from the patterns of her old life, such as volunteering at the library, courting new friends, and taking art classes at the local community college. Slowly, the calls and drop-ins became less frequent, and the volunteer manager opened her e-mail one afternoon and found that Julie was moving to another state to be near her daughter. She said she might consider volunteering for a nursing home in that town. The experience that Julie had with her nursing home volunteering and why she ended up leaving could not have been further apart. Her experience was positive, rewarding, and joyful, just as all of us would wish. Had circumstances stayed the same, she probably would have remained an outstanding volunteer for her nursing home. No amount of reassigning her duties, changing her role, or giving her time off would have made a difference. The building itself became a source of memory and pain. That could not be changed, so the only solution was for her to leave.

We can only hold on to volunteers as long as it works for them. Employees are paid and therefore must carefully consider leaving a job. Volunteers have the luxury of walking out at any given moment. So, the fact that volunteers come back week after week becomes almost miraculous when you stop and think about it. They don't come for the money. They don't typically come for the power. They don't normally come for recognition and praise. They come because it is meaningful, and because they have formed a lasting relationship with the mission and, in many cases, the volunteer manager. We nudge, foster, mentor, and encourage, but ultimately the volunteer forges the relationship that defines his/her experience. And sometimes, unfortunately, that relationship is not going to last very long. They get out of their volunteering what they need and then they are gone. Instead of faulting ourselves for their departure, we need to understand that they were not meant to be with us any longer than they had planned, whether they consciously knew it or not. We have to be able to let them go, to be grateful for the time they have spent with us. We have to recognize that we impacted their lives in a profoundly positive way on their journey by giving them the opportunity to grow. Our vulnerable charges are also better for having welcomed them into their lives.

The One That Got Away

Donald was newly retired and a volunteer who was at first a bit unsure. He had had a long career in civil service, and was not used to what he termed the "touchy-feely" aspect of hospice work, but he was determined to give it a try. His significant other had been volunteering very successfully at this particular hospice for many years and had finally convinced Donald that he should volunteer too. So Donald stuck his toe into the water by helping at fairs and functions. He was well-spoken, enthusiastic, charming, and had the ability to recruit other tentative people on the spot. He seemed to have a glow about him, and as he was always willing, the volunteer manager called him first and often. Slowly, Donald was introduced to patient care and he mentored with his wife, who was an experienced volunteer. He visited a patient on his own and did well. He visited another for a short time and then asked to be removed from the case. The volunteer manager assured him that another volunteer would be easily found and told him not to feel guilty. But the next assignment was turned down, and the next. Then Donald stopped returning phone calls and was never around to take any type of assignment. Puzzled and worried that someone had offended Donald, the volunteer manager cornered his wife one day and asked her if something was wrong. His wife sighed and said that Donald had started volunteering as a mentor in the public school system. He was also taking a class on victim advocacy and was becoming involved with children in the court system. The manager was intrigued yet puzzled, so she left another message asking him to call back to talk. This time, Donald did call back. He apologized profusely, saying that his actions were rude, but that he did not know how to quit. He sheepishly told her that his real passion was the court system and children who needed someone to help navigate the legal requirements. His many years as a mediator gave him the skills to excel at his new volunteer job. He promised that he would try to fill some shifts at an upcoming fair, but he never did. He simply moved on, having used the hospice volunteer experience as a stepping-stone. He was really looking for the right volunteer opportunity for him, and having just retired, he was willing to give the hospice a chance. But it never was the perfect fit for him, and when he found the one that did fit, he didn't look back. His wife continued to be a very good volunteer and brought Donald with her to all the social functions, where he would enthusiastically greet the volunteer manager and the volunteers he had come to know. He was obviously very happy in his new endeavor, as he would animatedly describe the children he was assigned to help. Hospice work was just not as fulfilling to him and nothing the volunteer manager could do would change that. The fact that Donald used hospice as a stepping-stone should be a source of pride, not a reason to feel as though his leaving was some type of failure. Donald gave as he learned and he moved forward. If a person who was working on getting his PhD decided to simply stay put after graduation, we would consider that odd or foolish. We learn and move on with our knowledge. Volunteers can do the same.

Gone Quickly

Jennifer was a brand-new volunteer for a home health group that prided itself on the integration of volunteers in the day-to-day operations of the organization. Jennifer had exceptional telephone skills and she happily agreed to call patients and families, asking if they would like to have a volunteer home health aide visit them in their homes. Her tender, sweet demeanor was exactly the soft approach that put family members at ease. Jennifer was extremely shy by nature, and the volunteer manager made sure to let her know how exceptional her work was, as well as making sure that all her questions were answered and she had all the tools she needed. After a few weeks, Jennifer's confidence increased and she settled into her volunteer assignment.

One day Jennifer came in for her regular shift to discover an unknown staff member using her usual desk and telephone. Jennifer was startled, but politely excused herself and went to look for the volunteer manager, who had to run an emergency errand. Not being assertive, Jennifer sat outside the office awaiting her turn at the desk. It did not come. When her allotted time was over, she went home. When the volunteer manager returned, she discovered Jennifer's work untouched and called her. After hearing what had happened, she apologized profusely and promised Jennifer that she would talk with the staff member who had been using the desk. The next week, Jennifer came in and gathered up her work. As she headed for the small work space, she saw a different staff member using her phone. Instead of finding the volunteer manager, she returned the work and quickly left. She called and quit the next day, giving an excuse about her schedule changing. She never mentioned the mix-up with the phone and desk, but simply said that she did not have the time to do the work. It wasn't until several weeks later that another volunteer, who knew Jennifer from church, learned the real reason and called the volunteer manager to let her know. By then it was too late to entice Jennifer back. Her shy and sensitive nature could not take being displaced twice, and she never would have had the fortitude to question a staff member.

Although her timidity was a plus when speaking to family members, it became her undoing in the end. While she was under the wing of the volunteer manager, she was all right. But that meant that the volunteer manager had to make sure she was present and available every time Jennifer came into the office. Eventually, there would be a time when Jennifer would be on her own. Something else might have made her quit. The sad truth is we can't protect our volunteers at all times from situations they deem unpleasant. Brusque staff, work not completely ready, changes in conditions, supervisors leaving due to an emergency, and continuous interruptions can cause some volunteers to leave. If they feel that conditions are not right for them, for whatever reason, they will tolerate the unpleasant situation only so long. We can't protect them from everything unless we are with them continually, and that defeats the purpose of having volunteers. Some just need a few weeks or months next to us before they are confident enough to navigate on their own. A handful, though, will never be able to stand the chaos of the non-profit office. They might be able to work later hours when the office is nearly empty, or take work home, but they cannot stand alone on their own two feet. The volunteer manager has to weigh whether or not the work the overly sensitive volunteer is doing is worth being chained to the office, answering questions, giving direction, and applauding each and every task accomplished. It may be worth it and it may not. If another volunteer can mentor the sensitive one, that may afford you the opportunity to break free while giving the shy volunteer the support he/she craves.

Gone in an Instant

David was a new volunteer who took orientation at a disaster relief organization and then went on a cruise around the world. Sometimes, volunteers want to get that training in before a major trip, or the schedule happens to fit perfectly, but not all volunteers start immediately after being trained. He patiently told the volunteer manager that he would call her when he got back and would then accept an assignment. When the volunteer manager did not hear from him after the allotted time passed, she called him. He told her that he had to fly to another state to help his daughter take care of a major move. David said he would call when he returned, but was not quite sure when that would be. Having never had the chance to really get to know David, the volunteer manager took him at his word, put his information in a drawer, and forgot about him. She thought that, based on their conversation, she would hear from him as soon as he was ready to begin his work. As she had been training volunteers for many years, she was used to situation after situation keeping some volunteers from starting for long periods of time.

A few weeks later, a marketing staff member called David from a list of prospective volunteers and asked him to help at a marketing event. David refused due to scheduling conflict, and went on to excoriate the volunteer department for letting him slip through the cracks. He complained that no one had checked on him or called him for job placement. The marketing specialist passed the message to the volunteer manager, who called David to apologize. He was not only annoyed, he adamantly complained about having to endure the lengthy orientation, only to be "cast aside." No matter the apology, the damage was done. David perceived the organization as fractured, disorganized, and lacking in communication. He most likely forgot that he had told the volunteer manager he would call when he was available to start.

This can be a common problem for new volunteers, who, having busy lives, take volunteer orientation but are unable to start immediately due to illness, scheduled surgery, trips, or moves. They may have the time to complete the training and have every intention of starting when they are able, but sometimes two or three circumstances prevent them from moving forward. When volunteers say they will call when ready, assume that they will not. Even if volunteers remember their promise to call, they will feel like we have forgotten them or don't need them if we do not check on them periodically. Juggling all the volunteers who need occasional "just checking in with you" calls is a daunting task. An office volunteer can be assigned to call other volunteers who are sick or on extended leave. If not a call, then a note in the mail or an e-mail message will at least show the volunteers that they are missed and wanted. Sometimes, we make mistakes that volunteers consider unforgiveable. At that point, you can try and call them periodically or learn from the small mistake that ended up being large in the volunteer's mind.

Chapter 3

What Did You Do with the Volunteer We Knew?

We all have special volunteers, those who are considered the cream of the crop, the ones we turn to practically every time we need something. They are the ones we trust with our most cherished projects, the ones we parade in front of the outside world and the inner world, because frankly, they won't screw things up by saying what they really think. They also won't share the time that we let them down, or showed our frustration in front of them, because they get it and are professional and kind enough to overlook the petty things other volunteers might not. They are the perennially best persons for the job. Actually, they are the best persons for all the jobs, and we wistfully claim that if we could only clone them, everything would fall into place. Maybe there is a volunteer ceiling, or perhaps there is a perfection life span, because these volunteers, when they fall, do so like a stone from a bridge because they were so high to begin with. Maybe we just expect too much from them. Maybe we get too comfortable around them. Maybe we pull them into our inner circle and let them view and be part of more than they can handle. Circumstances change. People change. Volunteers change. Being prepared for this can not only make us nervous, always looking over our shoulders, it can make us cynical. Bright lights burn out. Sometimes they fizzle with a little spark, and sometimes they just explode, showering debris all over us. It can happen with the best of volunteers. But why does it always seem to happen after they win a major award, or are interviewed for the newspaper, or are feted at an organizational extravaganza? It is a part of our job that is cruel and frustrating when we know that a certain formerly perfect volunteer is now removed from our list of volunteers for nefarious reasons. We smile politely when a staff member or another volunteer asks, "Where are Bill and Betsy? They're so wonderful; I just wonder if they are OK." At this point, which is the twentieth time we've been asked this question, we lie and say that Bill is taking some time off or Betsy is here somewhere. The sad truth is he ran amok; or, like a speeding freight train, we helplessly watched her derail. These events catch us so off guard that we wonder if they really happened. If you try to explain that to someone who does not work with volunteers, he/she will look at you like you have two heads. That sweet volunteer? There must be something wrong with the volunteer manager, not the volunteer. We must have done something to cause the problem. We overworked them, we didn't give them enough freedom, or we gave them too much. Sadly, we may have some culpability in their demise. It will, however, shake our faith in our ability to know and judge people.

The Big Change

I heard about Sally, a great volunteer for an organization that specializes in visiting shut-ins, especially the elderly. Sally was highly educated, well-spoken, and ready to tackle any assignment thrown at her. She mentored new volunteers. She worked closely with the staff, kept impeccable records, and always put the needs of her charges first.

Things changed for her, however. Her husband became ill, then died quickly, and she was lost, sad, and extremely angry. She started to depend on the volunteer staff. During her grieving, Sally looked to the volunteer department to be her rudder, to right her course which was spiraling out of control. As she had been a fixture in the inner circle of the organization, she looked to her friends and fellow workers to help her through the tough times. After all, her volunteering was the one spot free from the pain of losing her husband, the spot where she felt grounded, rewarded, and identified. While in bereavement, she insisted on continuing her visits with her shut-ins. The volunteer staff, after much thought, agreed to let her continue, and they promised each other that they would keep a watchful eye on her, for her own good and for the good of her charges. Sally began to take on more clients, and started helping at her church in her off hours. She heaped many responsibilities on herself and started to help an elderly neighbor as well.

She began to falter, letting little things slip. She didn't visit when she said she would. She forgot meetings. She arrived disheveled when dropping off reports at the office. Clearly, the volunteer staff was alarmed.

Sally began to criticize the running of the organization, in particular the volunteer department. She spoke to other volunteers about the "sloppy" practices. The volunteer staff delicately asked her if she was all right and she responded that she was a bit under the weather.

One day, Sally crossed a boundary by taking over the finances of one of her shut-ins. She moved his money to an account that she felt would better suit him, and paid off an outstanding loan he had taken out. She was immediately removed from the case. She argued with the staff over the wants and needs of the client. She went to the volunteer department, expecting them to rush to her defense.

When they did not, she lied about her involvement and threatened them with legal action. In short, she crashed and burned. The department was lucky her charge did not want to cause trouble and the episode was quickly forgotten. She left at the urging of the volunteer staff, who tried to counsel her, but failed to make her see what she had done wrong.

Volunteers' lives change. We all know they get sick, they move, they get married, they get a job, they retire, they lose a loved one, they start a business, they take in a family member, they travel, and sometimes they get into trouble. These life events can change the volunteer's perception of his work, commitment, and desire to be involved. We have to be very careful when circumstances change in our volunteers' lives. What happens in their personal life can affect their commitment to volunteering. We need to be ready for that. The question then becomes, at what cost are we willing to keep a volunteer who can no longer give our organizations what is needed? Even the best of volunteers may have a time limit on what they can do for us. It is a sad reality, but knowing that there is a shelf life to every volunteer may soften the blow. There just may not be anything you can do to change not only circumstances, but the way volunteers handle the changes in their lives. This journey is theirs and we can only mentor, encourage, and guide them throughout their volunteering. We can't orchestrate it.

Didn't See That Coming

Gwen was a volunteer I heard about who was in charge of a major project at her church. She was passionate about helping others, and felt that her church had the right attitude regarding giving back. It started a ministry to the sick program, and Gwen, a retired nurse, eagerly asked to head it up. She trained the core group of volunteers, put together a teaching manual, and developed a tracking system which ensured the program ran smoothly. She was a great spokesperson for the results of the project and often spoke during Sunday services, recruiting other parishioners to participate. Under her leadership, the ministry grew from the six original volunteers to a force of more than twenty well-trained individuals.

Gwen fell outside her condo one day and had to have emergency surgery. A widow, Gwen lived alone and needed help because her only relatives resided in another state. She turned to her ministry to the sick program volunteers. Unfortunately, without her at the helm, the program wasn't as efficient. The prescribed amount of volunteers came in when they were able to, but it wasn't enough in Gwen's eyes. She had given her heart and soul to the program, and now that she needed it, the extra help she felt she was entitled to wasn't readily available. Gwen became angry and spiteful, and when a volunteer did come to offer assistance, she berated him/her for taking so long to arrive. As her health improved, she reluctantly returned to church and to the program she had helped create. There, all were ecstatic to see her, but she quickly began to imagine that they only wanted her back to do the work. She was particularly ugly toward the minister, who had no clue as to Gwen's resentful feelings. Soon, Gwen grew distant and cold and gave excuses for not heading up the ministry to the sick program. The minister and other volunteers were helpless in the face of Gwen's extreme anger. They tried to make her feel wanted and needed, but one day she turned in all her materials pertaining to the program and coolly informed the minister that she was joining another church. No amount of cajoling would change her mind. She swiftly left.

How much do we owe a volunteer? This is one of those chicken-and-egg questions that really has no sound answer. We owe the volunteer the best volunteer experience possible, nothing more. Yet, when you look at the retention of volunteers, one of the main reasons volunteers stay is they feel connected to the mission and the work. Who in the heck is making them feel so connected? We are. What that means is, we are listening to their stories about their new grandchildren, we are calling them when they are sick, we are sending birthday cards, visiting them in the hospital, laughing with them, crying with them, holding their hand when tragedy strikes, and telling them how valuable they are. We are doing our job. Often, volunteer managers secretly wonder if they show favoritism. We do have our favorites, just like we have a favorite ice cream, favorite movie, and favorite place to spend a Sunday afternoon. That's just normal human behavior. Professionalism dictates that we treat all volunteers the same, but aren't there some that make you cringe and others you just want to hug? If you can try and make them all feel like they are the "good one," your rate of success will soar. But when a volunteer demands more than you can professionally give, or is not happy with the way you responded to her personal needs, then that is part of her problem, not yours. As cold as this sounds, we don't owe them everything and anything. We owe them a great volunteer experience. Everything else is above and beyond. If you are with them 100 percent when you are with them, you don't have to be with them 10 percent when you are with others. There are other volunteers too. And, we always have to ask, "What are you in this for? Are you here because you believe in the mission, or is there something personal that is driving you?"

Where Are You?

Another volunteer, Maggie—a widow, I was told—was a volunteer receptionist for a large organization that helped people get back on their feet after a devastating tragedy. She was professional, empathetic, and could listen longer to the folks that came in and with more compassion than any other volunteer and most staff members. She was so giving, so understanding, that when she met a new volunteer, Toni, who was being evicted from her apartment, Maggie took her in. Maggie felt that Toni needed a great deal of help. So began a saga of the wonderful volunteer that the volunteer department knew and counted on spending more time with and energy on a volunteer they hardly knew. Maggie became embroiled in a tangle of financial problems Toni insisted were not of her making. Maggie spent money on a lawyer for Toni and that alarmed the volunteer department. Although Toni had passed the background screening and all her references checked out, the department knew very little about her. Since Toni had just moved into the area from another state, there was little to go on, except a stinging gut feeling that Toni had observed Maggie's selfless giving and was taking full advantage of her kind nature. They tried to speak to Maggie about boundaries and trusting virtual strangers, hoping that she would see how she was being manipulated by Toni. They dug, but found no information on Toni that would back up their suspicions. The department had not observed anything unusual during Toni's initial interview, so had nothing concrete to present to Maggie. They could only speak to her about their growing suspicion that she was being taken advantage of. The department was powerless, because we all have to be especially careful when meddling in a volunteer's private affairs. They stood by helplessly and watched Maggie spend her money on Toni's problems. Eventually, Toni moved on after Maggie was not able to contribute any more financial help. Maggie kept in touch with Toni, and occasionally sent her money. She was disappointed that the volunteer department staff thought so little of Toni's predicament and felt they were coldhearted. She confided in another volunteer that she thought the volunteer managers were jealous of her relationship with Toni and were interested solely in her stellar volunteer accomplishments. Strained, the communication between Maggie and the volunteer department fractured quickly and she drifted away.

How much can we get involved in volunteers' personal lives? While we espouse giving our clients, patients, or charges choices, are we not bound to do the same for our volunteers? Or are we obligated to step in when we see them making mistakes? Sometimes they will ask for our help, sometimes they will not. And as we observe them making decisions we personally would not make, nor let our relatives make, we have to wonder: what is our role? This is very tricky, because we care about the volunteers' well-being, yet we are not in charge of their decisions. The fine line may lie in between, that space where we are there to listen, but not to give advice. It is hard when you see someone taking advantage of one of your volunteers.

What do you do with the volunteers you trust? Do you give them free rein? Do you respect them enough to leave them without monitoring? Do they come to your home? Do you invite them to family gatherings because they are alone? We seem to have a line drawn in the sand that we continually cross when we "like" the volunteer. After all, we make friends with fellow staff members, do we not? We hang out with them, become good friends with them, so what's the difference? Well, maybe we should look at it this way. Would you feel comfortable hanging out with your boss versus socializing with your peers? If you make a fool of yourself in front of your office mate, it's fodder for laughs on Monday morning. Make a fool of yourself in front of your boss and who knows next review time. Do you feel comfortable complaining about the workload with the executive director sitting at the table? It's not the same as clinking glasses with all the other worker bees.

We have to look at the volunteers as the worker bees and we are the bosses. Once we start sharing the inner circle with our volunteers, we've put them in the same position we would be in should we attend a casual party with administration. Oil and water don't mix well. Shake up the volunteers with the volunteer managers and eventually you could be in a precarious position. Just imagine bringing all your friends to work, giving them assignments, not paying them, and expecting them to act professionally. You have to be so careful not to overstep the boundaries with volunteers. They came to us for a reason, and that reason should be the continuing motivating factor, not the desire to please us personally, or the feeling that they are in the inner circle.

Nature Wins

Sometimes, leaving is not the volunteer's fault at all. How many of us have had volunteers who were absolutely wonderful, models of professionalism and examples of great behavior? They stay, thankfully, and become fully integrated into the system without overstepping their boundaries. They don't expect to be part of the inner circle, but look at their jobs with the same passion and understanding as we would hope. They were most likely excellent workers, and now they are excellent volunteers. You don't have to correct them, call them, or check on them. They don't expect much in return because they buy into the work and are happy to do it. They get so much from it.

So, what puts them in the category of what happened to you? Unfortunately, it has to do with frailty; with, dare I say it, aging; the breakdown of the mind and body. Some really great volunteers stay so long that you literally see them begin to fail right before your eyes. It's heartbreaking for us. It's heartbreaking for them. Some volunteers recognize that their repeated trips to the hospital spell physical decline. Some fortunate volunteers have loving children that are on top of their loved one's condition. And how fortunate for us when family members are already figuring out how to take care of Mom or Dad. They may naturally move in with a child, find a senior housing development to live in, or drift reluctantly away, no malice intended. They apologize for their frail behavior.

You assure them, with tears forming, that you still respect them and that they have so much to give. Unfortunately, there are those volunteers who do not have caring family. Children may live out of town. They may not be that involved. They may be lied to by the very volunteer who is declining. It then might become your problem. And oh, what a problem it is. The volunteer that greets people now looks unkempt, can't remember names, and makes obvious mistakes. The general public does not understand and therefore the volunteer becomes a liability. Who do you tell? How do you phrase it? Simply waiting for the volunteer to figure this out may never work. You have to take action and it is an unpleasant task. Do you call whatever family you know about?

I heard about a volunteer, Cara, who used to bring her husband with her when she volunteered. He had severe dementia and she could not leave him home alone. He was a wonderful man, and everyone knew how hard it was for Cara. Volunteering became her outlet. After a while, however, volunteers began to complain that they were babysitting Cara's husband. As much as they loved Cara, they did not sign up for that responsibility. Finally, after many weeks of avoidance, the problem could not be ignored any longer and the volunteer manager asked to see Cara. It turned out that she was grateful for the notice and had already realized the strain it was putting on her fellow volunteers. The volunteer manager was flabbergasted. She had expected the conversation to go badly. She was fortunate. It won't always go that way. The family may resent your intrusion. They may not want your input and feel that you are being unfair. They may not want to face the situation. The volunteer may balk, get mad, and feel patronized. It is a very tricky road. Treading lightly is the first step. Obviously, you are not going to go up to a volunteer and very loudly announce, "Bob, you are losing it! You can't even get the name of our executive director right! You are scaring the people that come here. And your clothes are dirty!" We all have much more tact than that—although I knew a volunteer coordinator who once told a volunteer that she was "not the brightest bulb in the Christmas tree display."

If volunteers were employees, it would be a different story. Sure, we can have all the performance evaluations we want, but the truth is this volunteer gave years of faithful service. We don't want to crush him/her. Volunteers deserve better. Chances are you feel like they are akin to your aunt or uncle. And who wants to hurt Auntie Polly or Uncle Charlie? So, we make excuses for them, help them much more than we did before and keep our eye on them, redoing their work if necessary. We care. And every time they faithfully come in, we think about having that uncomfortable conversation with them. Should we call their children, mention the stain on the formerly spotless polo shirt? Should we mention the uncombed hair on the back of their head? Do we sit them down and explain that they ask the same question over and over? We once had a patient who called and said that she had met the volunteer, and although she appreciated having her come out, she didn't want her to come anymore. The reason? The volunteer seemed older and frailer than the patient. Tell that to the volunteers who would go on doing the work until they couldn't get out their door anymore.

Sometimes, we kindly try to create a harmless do-nothing job for the volunteers and we lie to them, telling them that we need their help elsewhere. Occasionally, we get very lucky and the volunteer recognizes his/her declining state. At times they do not, and we are forced to keep escorting them into the building, parking their cars, or sitting by them as they try to do their work. It is this aspect of volunteer management that is not management at all. It is simply caring. No one wants to be told that he/she is no longer useful. We can't bring ourselves to do it, so we help them retain their dignity for as long as they are able, letting nature be the one to guide us and them.

I want you to imagine a manufacturing company that sends a manager out every day to take an older employee by the elbow and guide him to his workbench. Then the manager sits patiently with this older employee and helps him do his work. When the day is over, the manager helps him to his car, thanking him for coming in and reiterating how much they appreciate him. At first we might say, "Awww," and then, after a moment, we would shake our heads and wonder, how on earth could this company survive? Luckily, our volunteer doesn't come in for a forty-hour workweek, so we can survive. Of course, we may have several of these volunteers, so do the math. A portion of our time is spent tidying up after them. But is their usefulness gone? Have they reached their shelf life through no fault of their own?

Having seasoned volunteers speak to new volunteers is a wonderful way to give them a chance to pass on their passion and history. Having them mentor new volunteers if only on the phone creates usefulness. After all, if the new volunteer is going to be kind and patient with our clients, then what better way to show it than with an aging fellow volunteer? Human resources are about the best people for the job. Volunteer management is that and more. We exist in a world more in gray shades than black and white. Whereas employment does not have to take the feeling of the employed into consideration, volunteer management is all about the feeling of the volunteer. We have to juggle the volunteer's "pay" with the needs and wishes of the organization. There is no "it's part of your job, deal with it" in our vocabulary. So, recognition, respect, and retention become the triple R of volunteer leadership. Little white lies go a long way in our profession. We say, "No, it wasn't that the client didn't like you, they just decided to hire someone," or, "We really need someone with your talent and skills in a more important area," or, "I was just going to call you for that special assignment when another volunteer walked in and wanted to do it." Can you imagine doing that with an employee? If we were always brutally honest, we would have a lot less volunteers. But, can we not tactfully tell volunteers the truth? Can we not say, "It wasn't that the client didn't like you, they just felt that the other volunteer's personality fit better with their needs," or, "We felt your skills were better suited for a different job," or, "I had someone else in mind for that assignment, but I do have something for you if you're interested." We don't have to hurt anyone's feelings, but we also don't have to give the impression that volunteers are perfect and can do anything they feel like doing. We are charged with providing the best volunteer for the job and we are more professional when we show that we actually give a great deal of thought to assigning a volunteer. Volunteers do appreciate professionalism over spineless praise. Being tactful yet honest does not equate to being mean.

Chapter 4

Maybe You Shouldn't Be Here Anymore

Too Long

Sandy had been a volunteer for more than twenty years at a large hospital. She had outlasted any volunteer director and most volunteers. She was a fixture. Fixtures have a certain mystique about them, an untouchable aura that keeps criticism at bay. If volunteers have lasted that long, the theory goes, they must be good. They are seasoned, they are knowledgeable. The truth is volunteers only know as much as we tell them. If there are very few ways to impart information to volunteers, or if they refuse to attend important meetings, they are not informed. If the volunteers start to act independently, and have their own untouchable position in the organization, they may be insulated from the latest updates on policy and procedural changes. They may not be hearing the message. They may not be as knowledgeable as the volunteer who just came out of orientation. As a matter of fact, their knowledge may be twenty years old and fading. Their reality may be the reality they have created, and since they have such tenure, no one dares to check to see if the volunteers are really acting within the parameters of the organization. It may have been perfectly acceptable for a volunteer to be involved in a patient's business twenty years ago, before you got there, but it is not acceptable today. Does the volunteer realize that, or is he/she operating on twenty-year-old knowledge? It may be difficult to challenge a volunteer who has been there longer than you. You may feel like the volunteer should know more than you do because he/she has many more years of experience. In reality, that volunteer may have developed really bad habits over the course of twenty years and no one had the guts to do something about it. It may fall upon you to straighten out those volunteers who have run amok. Volunteers like to feel valued. One way to feel valued is by teaching others about a subject. So, we can ask the long-term volunteers to teach us about the way things were done in the "old days," but with one caveat. Things are not done that way today. Ask them to explain how they have adjusted to the change and they might surprise you by admitting they know change has come. But if they talk about the ways things are done with flawed, outdated ideas, you may have to have a heart-to-heart talk with them, a task that is not easy. These volunteers may not take correction well. They may scoff, argue, stomp out, treat you like a naïve youngster, and ask how you dare to question their long service. You may find yourself on the defensive. Having policies written and presented regularly is the key to establishing any changes. Volunteers must review and sign these policies. Successful volunteers are able to change with the times in order to best support the organization they respect and work for.

But back to Sandy. She always walked into the hospital wing with the aplomb of a famous surgeon, I was told. She had been married to a physician and carried the weight of his importance with her as she reported for her regular Wednesday duties. Sandy felt on par with the staff, including the physicians, and would offer her expert opinion on patients, inserting her opinions into clinical conversations.

She often went to upper management with her concerns. Staff would sigh and tolerate her involvement, but never do anything about her unacceptable behavior. Because Sandy was married to a physician, the volunteer director did not feel that she could counsel Sandy or remove her from her volunteering. So, Sandy became a nuisance to be tolerated rather than a helpful presence. Sandy was in it for her own edification and sense of importance, patients be damned. Sandy never attended volunteer meetings. She felt she did not need to. She did not ask questions of the volunteer director, her immediate supervisor. She felt she knew more. This can be a dangerous situation for the volunteer staff. When a volunteer operates outside the rules, it is akin to letting a driverless car speed toward an eventual crash. Someone needs to have the courage to stop the runaway vehicle. If someone like Sandy refuses to attend meetings, that can be a violation of your rules, should you choose to require volunteers to attend them. There really isn't much that could be done about her attitude except have a heart-to-heart with her. Changes could have been received better if the volunteer director had sat down with Sandy and several of the clinical staff. Having the staff present shows solidarity and a shared message within the organization.

Do we need to take volunteers like Sandy down a peg? Not necessarily, but we do have to put the needs of her patients above her personal need to be in charge. Does Sandy need to feel important? Is there another way to give her that feeling without harming the program? For a time, the volunteer director asked Sandy to speak to new volunteers, but she abandoned that idea after listening to Sandy go on and on about her own accomplishments rather than giving helpful information. Eventually, Sandy quit due to a health issue. Everyone breathed a sigh of relief when she left, but years of tolerating Sandy could have been avoided by not treating her as untouchable.

Between a Rock and a Hard Place

Julia was a sharp lady who enthusiastically joined the volunteer force at an organization that cared for low-income families. She was a talkative, animated volunteer who was a perfect fit for the young children that were being helped in this program. Julia did an excellent job of reporting her activities and turned in her paperwork on time. She rarely called off and had one of the best rates of attendance in her families' homes. She took advantage of as many educational opportunities as her schedule permitted.

One day, a family member forgot to pick up her child at school, leaving the eight-year-old stranded for over an hour. Julia criticized that family member in front of the rest of the family, who then complained to the case worker. Julia was removed from the case immediately and another volunteer was assigned. Julia felt that she was unfairly blamed for simply pointing out the family member's lack of judgment. Her main interest, she reasoned, was the children's care, and she felt that they needed to be protected. While speaking to the family, the volunteer manager found out that Julia had criticized them on numerous occasions.

The volunteer manager patiently explained to Julia that it was better for the family, and better for her as a volunteer, to refrain from going back into that home. Since she had no other clients, she became stuck on that family and their perceived unfair criticism of her. She badgered the volunteer manager about the family and wanted to know why they would malign her in that way. Again and again, the manager tried to explain that the fit was not good, and even if the family was completely wrong about the situation, it still was best to remove Julia from the assignment. Julia went to upper management with her story. She reminded upper management that her husband had donated a sizeable amount of money to the organization upon his death. She even hinted that more money would be left to it upon her death. Pressure was exerted on the volunteer manager to "make a place" for Julia. By this time, the volunteer manager wondered if she ever really knew Julia at all. Her attitude was shocking. The manager began to seriously doubt her own ability to place volunteers. If a seemingly good volunteer like Julia turned out to be a poor one, how many other volunteers were out there doing harm? Julia obeyed and did not go back to the family she had criticized. She was given several assignments interviewing families before they came into the program, but she never let go of the family that "turned her in." She became a complaining, unreasonable volunteer. The manager called her less often, didn't return her calls immediately, and started to wean her away. It worked. She grew bored or tired of waiting and stopped volunteering.

The manager's hands were tied in this instance. Julia's donation trumped any remedial action, so the manager was forced to walk on eggshells while trying to do the best job she could, considering she had to deal with a volunteer forced upon her. Julia's shelf life ended not when she criticized the family, but when she became stuck on the family that complained about her. Volunteers can be rehabilitated, but they must be cognizant of their actions.

This manager was forced to endure Julia longer than she should have. Sometimes, we have to endure certain volunteers for varied reasons. They may be members of a higher-up's family. They may have given money. They may threaten a lawsuit for some reason. These are the volunteers that should be gone, but are not. Their motivations are harmful and their ability to further the mission nonexistent. Our clients, however, should not suffer as a result, and it is our ethical duty to protect our vulnerable charges. Explain to your superiors why you will not place a volunteer with helpless families. Present supporting documentation. Tell them you are willing to grin and bear it and give the volunteer in question a desk job. If that fails, at least you are on record as advocating for your clients.

You Must Be Joking

Steve was a volunteer who joined the thrift shop of an organization that cared for people with a rare disease. He spoke to the manager of the shop, telling him that he wanted to help raise funds for the organization, because his mother had suffered horribly from this disease many years before. Being newly retired, he said he was strong, willing to help in any way he could, and wanted to see the shop thrive. Steve began working five days a week at the shop. He spent most of the day there, receiving items, fixing electronics, and helping customers take purchases to their vehicles.

It wasn't long after Steve started that the shop manager noticed the other volunteers avoiding Steve. He started to question them individually and heard the same story from each one. Steve had a ferocious temper and would fly off the handle at any given moment. The volunteers were genuinely afraid of Steve. They told the shop manager that he had waved his fist at one or two of them while in the back room. Shocked, the shop manager called Steve into the office and had a talk with him. Steve assured him that the other volunteers were exaggerating and did not like him. He said he didn't want to get them in trouble, but he had caught several of them taking items and they were fearful that he would expose them.

Thoroughly confused, the shop manager kept a watchful eye on everyone. As his confusion deepened, he happened to run into the volunteer manager from one of the offices. This manager placed volunteers who would drive the ill patients to their doctor's appointments. The shop manager started to tell his story about Steve, hoping to get some good advice from this long-term volunteer manager. To his complete surprise, she not only knew Steve, but had dismissed him from taking any patients to their appointments. It seems that Steve had gotten angry with a patient who was late getting ready to see the doctor. He had caused quite a scene in her office when she terminated him and security had been summoned.

She apologized profusely for not informing the shop manager, but in truth it had never occurred to her that Steve would try another volunteer avenue. Suddenly, it all made sense to the shop manager and he enlisted the help of the volunteer manager and security to fire Steve. Luckily, Steve had signed an agreement statement placing him on a six-month probationary period. That signed agreement made the firing go smoothly.

Unfortunately, many wonderful thrift shop volunteers had had to endure Steve's wrath. It was quite a few weeks before things settled down, but with patience, the shop returned to normal.

All of this could have been avoided had the volunteer manager informed each and every other volunteer manager about Steve. Even problem prospective volunteers' information should be shared with anyone who might come in contact with them. It's often harder to fire a volunteer once he/she is accepted.

Many volunteer managers who stay in their jobs for a length of time can recount inappropriate prospective volunteers calling every two years, hoping that the manager has changed. Some people do not take no as an answer very well. We have to be very careful not to let those who are wrong for our organization find a way in. But we also have to be very careful in the verbiage we use when sharing that information with other volunteer managers. Calling a prospective volunteer "crazy" could backfire if he/she gets wind of it. We have to be concrete and professional about our assessments, and any written record should reflect only pertinent facts, quotes, and observations.

There is a debate about how often volunteers can and should volunteer. In Steve's case, he volunteered many hours. We often get desperate and will take whatever help is offered. Generally, how-ever, a new volunteer's burnout rate is much higher when he/she works as many hours as a part-time or full-time employee. The vol-unteers who successfully work many hours are those who begin slowly; then, as they get comfortable and enjoy what they are doing, increase their hours gradually. Too many good volunteers, when allowed to work twenty or more hours a week up front, become resentful and embroil themselves in the minutia of the work. This guarantees they will feel like unpaid laborers and will quickly burn out and leave.

Shouldn't Have Let You in the First Place

Ben was the thirteen-year-old son of a staff member at a large hos-pital. As the staff member did not want her son to be alone all sum-mer during his time off from school, she approached the volunteer director, asking that Ben be allowed to volunteer. The minimum age for volunteering at this hospital was fifteen, but the staff mem-ber assured the volunteer director that he was "mature for his age" and eventually wanted to study medicine. The volunteer manager, who had worked with this staff member in a previous position, against her better judgment accepted the young man into the vol-unteer program. Ben took the student orientation and soon began to show up at the volunteer director's office every other day looking for something to do. The staff member was bringing Ben in with her every day, trying to keep him busy herself; finding that she could not, she encouraged him to find the volunteer director to see "if there was something that needed to be done." Ben soon grew bored working on the computer, filing papers, and stuffing envelopes. He quickly exhausted the jobs available for young people. Even though Ben did say he was interested in becoming a physician, the volunteer director deemed him too immature to work directly with the patients. Unfortunately, the volunteer director did not feel comfortable telling his mother that it was unacceptable to drop her son off essentially to be babysat by the volunteer department. She struggled every day that Ben appeared. She made up work for him to do, spent time working with him on projects that were unnecessary and, due to his presence, fell behind in her work. Because Ben grew bored and tired of being forced to volunteer at his mother's place of business, he started to wander around the building when the volunteer director was not paying attention. She would find him in the lunchroom, or sitting outside, or making phone calls out by the lobby. This young man became a time-consuming chore and she could have kicked herself for allowing him to come three and four days a week. However, because she had not addressed the problem originally, she felt that she could not do so now without a good reason—other than that the arrangement was driving her crazy. One day, Ben wandered away again. The volunteer director took a walk to look for him and was unable to find him. She looked in all his haunts. Figuring he went to join his mother, she dropped by her office. He was not there. Panicked, the volunteer director took another thorough look around and had to inform his mother that Ben was missing. It seemed that he had arranged to meet a couple of his friends who walked to the hospital where, accompanied by Ben, they headed for the nearest fast-food restaurant. His mother was furious, the volunteer director was blamed, and policy was then written. The manager, although she had reprimanded Ben numerous times for leaving the department area, was considered at fault. It didn't matter that she had put up with babysitting a teen. It didn't matter that she bent over backward to help a fellow staff member, and it made no difference that she was overworked. She was at fault. It took some time for the volunteer director to get over her anger at not only Ben and his mother, but at the unfair treatment she felt she had received. From that incident, however, grew a series of rules and regulations for teen volunteers. The department formalized their teen program, came up with stringent guidelines and stuck to them. It made the next group of teens much easier to manage. It was really unfortunate that this volunteer director went through that experience, but it was a learning one and it could have been so much worse. At times we set aside our rules and our better judgment to help someone out. It may be that a person needs community service, or an acquaintance needs a favor, or another staff member needs us to just make an exception. We have all done it and vowed never to do it again. We do learn from our mistakes, and that is how policies are formed. It is not that we can't trust anyone; it is that when our gut tells us not to make an exception, we should listen and obey. We don't really have the time to stretch the rules so far as to cause us extra work and heartache. It's ultimately better to stick to the rules, as they are there to protect us. People just have to understand that we cannot make exceptions. Teens can be a joy and a blessing to work with, but they have a short attention span. When dealing with teens, make sure that they are not being dropped off at your place because they have nowhere else to go. They, too, need to be there for the right reason, and can learn much from their volunteer experience. Before you accept teens, think about interviewing them and their parent or guardian to get a sense of what they want out of their stint with you. Explain the rules during that interview and have the parent sign off on them. Don't hesitate to tell a teen to call his parent to come get him when his time is up. It is not your responsibility to make busywork for him.

Where Did That Come From?

Marty was a volunteer for a small hospice. She visited at a nursing home where she did some amazing things with the patients. She was particularly adept at engaging patients with limited memory and she became a favorite of the nursing home staff. Marty had a bubbly personality, having spent many years teaching preschool. She often compared working with elderly patients to her days of working with young children. She treated everyone with deep respect. Because she was quick-witted, creative, and versed in teaching, she had free rein in the nursing home and mentored any new volunteers that came on board. Marty would entertain the newcomers with tales of her favorite patients and they learned much from her innovative ideas. One day, Marty was talking to a new class of hospice volunteers and someone asked her opinion on the rights of elderly patients. Marty went off on a tangent about her views on the elderly, their rights, and the legislation surrounding that issue. It was a bit odd, but the volunteer manager noted that the class did not seem fazed by it. The next time Marty spoke to a class, she brought up the same subject without prompting and expounded on political issues as well as patients' rights. By now, the volunteer manager was perplexed and concerned. After the class, she spoke to Marty about the direction of her talk and Marty admitted that she was becoming involved in local politics. The manager reminded Marty that politics was one of those taboo subjects and Marty assured him that she was not discussing politics with patients. However, one afternoon, the son of a patient Marty visited regularly called the volunteer manager to complain that Marty had left a book with his mother. The book was a highly polarizing political best seller that appealed to one particular opinion. The son and his mother were of the opposing opinion, and he was very upset that a volunteer would try to convert his poor captive mother in such an underhanded way. The volunteer manager apologized profusely, and then called Marty. She was unapologetic, proudly recounted that she had started attending a local political action group, and berated the volunteer manager for his intolerance of her newfound passion. He warned Marty, telling her that another incident such as the book foisted on a patient and he would have to let her go. She sniffed haughtily, told him that he had no right to interfere in her private affairs, and reminded him that she had taken many a difficult assignment for their hospice. Two weeks later, the charge nurse at the nursing home called with a complaint. Marty had brought literature into the nursing home and was distributing it to the staff. Again the volunteer manager called Marty, hoping that the story was not true. Marty had been waiting for his call, because in a rehearsed statement, she coolly informed him that she was not discussing politics with the patients. At that point, the volunteer manager admitted that he lost it. He angrily told Marty that her services were no longer needed and demanded that she return her badge. He then called the team, and the nursing home to tell them that Marty was no longer a hospice volunteer. Losing our temper with a volunteer is never good. Sometimes, we do get very upset with them, but we always must remain professional in our approach. He was correct to fire her, because the nursing home staff is every bit as much a client as the patient and his/her family. Isn't it puzzling when volunteers goad us, knowingly defy us, or defiantly challenge us? It happens, and we wonder what type of personality takes pleasure in that behavior, especially after having received praise, guidance, and kindness from us. Enforcing the rules while soothing egos is one of the hardest parts of our jobs. How much do you have to take from a volunteer before you say, enough? A great number of people perceive that volunteers are untouchable; that when the offer of help is given, it must be accepted, respected, and submitted to without question. Volunteers behaving badly not only undermine the organizational mission, they undermine your authority. Insubordination should be a terminable offense. Be careful, though, and make it a formal termination. Give the volunteer the chance to defend his/her position, have more than one person present in the room, and allow the volunteer to leave with dignity. If you can point to specific rules that have been broken, instead of simply claiming a bad attitude, then the termination will be understandable and professional.

Chapter 5

So Many Reasons, Aren't There?

In all levels of the workplace people bemoan the fact that what they do can only be understood by those who also do it. That's why peer group meetings are so successful. It's helpful to be around others who actually have experienced what you have experienced, who do not talk down to you but talk with you, who can smile knowingly when you recall the crazy things that happen on occasion. This is the complaint—or lament, if you will—that really resonates in the volunteer world. How many managers, other staff members, or outsiders who, once they actually spend a bit of time within your department, say to you, "Seriously, I couldn't do what you do," and you know they mean it.

Have you had volunteers over the course of the years work directly in your office? Are they continually amazed at how difficult volunteer management can be, and do they shake their heads and ask, "How do you do it?" Recently, a volunteer manager said to me that when she entered the field, she thought that she would be working with sweet little elderly ladies all day long. How hard could that be? Is this the image that we project? Do those who are not privy to our jobs think we simply ask little old ladies, who have no other agenda but to please, to do our bidding and presto, it's done? We know how far from reality that is.

So what makes us stay? As any volunteer manager who has lasted longer than six months knows, it's not the pay. It's definitely not the recognition. It's not the hours. It's not the ease of the job. It's not the glamour. It's not the standard anything.

Who else would work for low pay, yet manage great numbers of unpaid workers? Who else would spend long hours on the phone with volunteer after volunteer and then head home with no easily measurable work done? Who else would have great ideas and then patiently wait for the right volunteer to come along to implement those ideas?

We are a breed unto our own. We see clearly the greatness of our work. We see clearly the good we heap upon society. We see clearly the tremendous amount of effort it takes to get one small project off the ground and then revel quietly on the profound results.

A volunteer manager at large hospital complex once told me an annoying story. She was in her office consoling a volunteer who had just learned that her husband of fifty years had lung cancer. This woman was one of those great volunteers who quietly go about doing their work, never looking for any recognition. She came to see the volunteer manager because they had formed a strong bond over the years. She needed to be able to freely express her sadness, and alternately cried and talked. Without warning, a member of administration, who was attending a meeting next door, opened the door without knocking. The administrator needed something right then and, looking at the volunteer and the volunteer manager with exasperation, announced, "I need you right now," and closed the door. The volunteer apologized for taking up valuable time and left. The bond and moment were broken. You know, of course, that the member of administration did not need anything of importance.

Now, here's the interesting question. Would that same administrator have burst into the surgical office and interrupted a family member tearfully recounting the illness and impending surgery of a loved one? Yet here was a volunteer whose husband would most likely avail himself of the surgical services at that hospital. Volunteers must be viewed by our organizations as more than just labor. They are clients, donors, marketing people, referral sources, and so much more. If the volunteers are out there talking up the organizations they volunteer for, it is likely more than the mission they are grateful for. It's the treatment they are receiving while volunteering, and the volunteer manager in nearly all instances is responsible for that.

People who do not work in our field seldom understand that volunteer managers are counselors, grief experts, best friends, daughters, sons, cousins, travel agents, relocation specialists, case managers, transporters, mentors, education specialists, and a host of other professions that are needed to assist our volunteers.

When an employee needs assistance, there are usually programs in place to help him/her. Where does a volunteer go for assistance? The volunteer manager. We have a role unlike any other in human resources. We become every department rolled into one. And we do it for twice, sometimes three times as many part-time, unpaid employees.

Ask a member of your management team to imagine that all his/ her employees suddenly became volunteers. Which ones would be kept? Which ones would be really, really hard to work with? Which ones are there for the right reasons? Which ones would quit? Ask that same manager if he/she could treat the employees all the same now that they are volunteers. Ask him/her to imagine that all those employees turned volunteers only worked between three and ten hours per week, and that there were now three times as many to manage. Ask him/her to think about the employees turned volunteers who now did not have to show up for work. How might his/her managerial style change?

Now ask the manager to imagine not having the human resources programs to support those employees turned volunteers. Tell him/her that he/she alone had to manage every aspect of these volunteers; that there would be no middle managers, no traditional support. How would his/her day-to-day change?

Explaining volunteer services is a gargantuan task. A lot of folks say "herding cats" and then we all laugh, and still no one gets it. We have to be able to make people understand the complexities of what we do. Analogies sometimes work.

Imagine there are two employees and they both have a task at hand to fill. We are going to give them decks of cards that represent people to do the tasks. Give employee one a deck of cards. Give employee two three decks of cards. Employee two certainly has the advantage, doesn't he? Employee one has the cards laid out in front of him. Each card has the same value (number of hours an employee works). Employee two has cards with all sorts of values (volunteers work varied amounts of hours). Employee one has cards that line up into neat suits (staff member jobs). Employee two has random suits, with some cards fitting into more than one slot (volunteer jobs are so varied). Employee one has cards that have to fit within the scope of the task (paychecks). Employee two's cards can do whatever they want (no paycheck). Employee one's tasks always lie within the scope of what his cards are slotted to do (staff jobs are defined). Employee two is given random tasks (volunteer requests) because the cards don't fit into any particular slot. Does employee two really have the advantage? Employee two has many more cards, and why wouldn't the cards do a task? They have no slot anyway. For example, why can't they drive a client's daughter who is bipolar to her weekly therapy. Employee one, when given a task, simply picks a card from the appropriate suit and assigns the task. Employee two, when given a task, has to sort through all the random cards, figuring out which card can best do the task, which card is actually available, and which card will take the least amount of effort to convince that it should do the task. Employee one might have to pick one of two cards to get the task done. Employee two may have to pick between five and twenty cards before finding one to do the task. Employee one can go back to finding other cards for the next task. Employee two has to commiserate with the first card he picked because the first card doesn't see the value in driving the daughter to weekly therapy because there are three people in the house who are perfectly capable and they refuse to drive the daughter, and the first card did not sign up to do work that wasn't meaningful. So employee two finds a second card, but that card will be on vacation next week, so it will do the task this week only. So employee two finds card three to do the task the following week, but now the daughter has changed her day and card three can't do it that day. Employee two finds card four, but card four's car is going to be serviced on week three, so employee two finds card five, but that card has relatives coming to town. Can card five take the relatives with her when transporting the daughter? And while card five has employee two on the phone, can employee two help card five move some items out of her house when he has the time? If you had to read that last part more than twice to understand it, chances are you're not a volunteer manager.

Oops, We Should Have Told You

Ted volunteered for an organization that had multiple regional offices. He was a prompt volunteer and did clerical work, envelope stuffing and occasional phone tree calling for the organization. Ted was very reliable, one of the dependable volunteers that made the busy office hum. He came in once a week for four hours at a time. Ted had been volunteering at the office for more than ten years and was a welcome fixture. One day, Ted did not come to work and did not call in, which was unlike him. The volunteer manager called Ted at home to see if he was all right. Ted answered and apologized for not letting the manager know, but he had decided to stop volunteering. Perplexed and worried, the volunteer manager tried to get Ted to open up and talk, to no avail. Ted thanked her for the many years he had had at the office and said good-bye.

The next day several of the office staff inquired about Ted, as they did not see him the day before. Reluctantly, the volunteer manager informed them that Ted had resigned, and secretly she wondered if Ted had become ill. The staff was also puzzled as to why Ted left and what the reasons could be for his sudden departure. One staff member, after overhearing the conversation, asked to see the volunteer manager privately. When they were behind closed doors, the staff member explained that Ted had applied for a job that was posted a month before, an opening for a part-time secretary. Ted, having been part of the office for so many years, felt he had the knowledge about the inner workings of the organization to be a very good secretary. The problem was, Ted knew the people in the offices and certainly knew about the good work that was being done, but he had no secretarial experience, no computer skills, and not much phone etiquette. The newly hired secretary had started the week before he left. Upon further investigation, the volunteer manager discovered that no one took Ted aside and explained why he had not been hired. He was simply ignored. Ted may have had unrealistic expectations about being hired due to the warm and friendly atmosphere of the office. The volunteer manager wondered if Ted would have kept volunteering had someone explained to him why he didn't get the job. The manager wished she had known about the job application, wished Ted had told her, but as that did not happen, the incident was out of her hands. Unfortunately, we cannot control each moment a volunteer is with us. All staff within our organizations must have the same consideration and concern for the volunteers as we do. It is a philosophy that must be taken seriously by everyone who works with us, so that volunteers are treated as a valuable resource worth cultivating and keeping. It is not only our job, but the entire organization's as well. Volunteers are smart enough to know when the volunteer department is the only source of thanks and praise.

The shelf life of a volunteer certainly varies. It may be immediate, because we deem the volunteer unsuitable for the work, or it might be natural, as when a volunteer moves, becomes ill, or has a change in status. A volunteer, though, may have several shelf lives within your organization. Some volunteers will go away for a period of time and then return later. I once had a volunteer who came back eight years later. I recently had a volunteer come back after a twelve-year absence. She had a very stressful job that she retired from and remembered her positive volunteer experience from before; as she now has the time, she wants to do the work she started twelve years ago.

Sometimes, volunteers have no idea that they will not last. They have every good intention. They may have been helped by your organization and want to return the kindness. They may think of the spiritual growth potential, or may just have a big heart. But you can almost tell the minute you meet them that unfortunately they will not last. They are keyed up, busy, scattered a bit, involved in so many things, from jobs to family to other commitments. They seem to flit as you speak to them, their wings ready to carry them off to the area that needs them the most at the moment. These volunteers have the shortest of shelf lives. They want to be with you, volunteering, doing good work, but they can't. They can't commit to a schedule and they can't fill in on short notice. They want to volunteer, but they don't have the time, not really. So, their own good intentions can't save them. They constantly tell you no, but ask you to call again. Eventually, after offering every volunteer job and every conceivable schedule to them, you give up. You stop calling. They don't call you either and they drop off. You may check in with them periodically, but all you get is their answering machine, and if you ever speak with them, they are embarrassed and hurry you off the phone. At that point, all you can do is remember their good intention and hope that they return when the time is right for them. You can send them occasional greeting cards if you feel that they will someday be right for your mission. You can keep them in the back of your mind or on a list, and when something new or special comes up, you can call those volunteers. It works more often than not. Recently, I heard of a volunteer named Inez, who had tried to do the jobs that were offered, but couldn't. She painfully explained that she thought the shelter she volunteered for was right for her, but couldn't bring herself to do the actual work. She really wanted to help, but emotionally could not. She left, but the very astute volunteer manager kept thinking about Inez and her desire to help. They had once had a conversation about gardening, something Inez enjoyed doing at home. When the shelter looked into creating a butterfly garden, the volunteer manager immediately called Inez, who was thrilled to be able to do something that was not only very helpful, but right for her personality and state of mind. It worked. Gathering as much information as you can on volunteers' hobbies and interests can one day prove very helpful. Newsletters offering new opportunities will catch those volunteers who might have just developed a new passion, or would like a change or want to try something more advanced. The number-one reason people volunteer is that they were asked. We always need to be prepared to ask everyone, because the person who says yes is oftentimes surprising. These are the volunteers who have not yet reached their shelf life. They may change focus, may need to take a lengthy sabbatical, or may stop for an extended period of time. They may eventually be the volunteers whose end comes naturally due to age, moving, or inability to continue. They are the volunteers that don't quite fit into the traditional roles you offer. It may take a long time for them to find their niche or their rhythm, but they are willing to stick around until that happens. There are always going to be certain volunteers that exist on the edges of organizations. They will be there to help when they can, but their journey is slow and spotty. You call them periodically and they appreciate it more than most, because they feel that you should give up on them. You make them feel special, because you tell them that you have faith in them and that your organization truly wants their help. All that faith and encouragement strengthens their loyalty and eventually you reap the benefits.

It Couldn't Be Helped

Janice came to a volunteer department at a women's shelter after she tried many different organizations. She was a highly intelligent woman, a business owner's wife who helped her husband with payroll and belonged to many social and philanthropic groups. Someone dear to her had been abused and had found help and solace at the women's shelter, and Janice was impressed with the caring individuals who ran the organization. She deposited herself at the volunteer department door with humble thanks and great expectations. The volunteer manager, sensing the deep potential in this prospective volunteer, patiently took slow, calculated steps to cultivate Janice's interest in helping the mission. It was obvious that Janice could bring talents, passion, contacts, funding, and recruits to the organization. The manager, with high hopes, spent a great deal of time mentoring Janice and accommodated her schedule and preferences. Janice was hooked. This very smart volunteer manager had recognized the great potential in Janice and was willing to do the up-front work to realize that potential. The experience turned out to be rewarding for both Janice and for the department, as Janice slowly learned to work with abused women. In turn, she brought donations, contacts, and other women into the program. After a year or so, Janice felt comfortable enough with the organization to increase her volunteering to several drop-in times a week. She served on advisory boards and chaired a volunteer action committee that was responsible for initiating community awareness.

One afternoon, Janice came into the volunteer manager's office and tearfully told her that she had to cut back on her volunteering. Her husband's business had lost several major contracts due to a slowdown in the economy and he had to lay off a number of workers. That meant she now had to work many more hours helping him with the business. It was tragic, because Janice had just reached her stride and was on her way to changing the way her organization viewed volunteer involvement. Unfortunately, Janice never volunteered again. Her progress, intentions, and love for the mission could not overcome the hard financial times. Although Janice could not give any more of her time, she remained a vocal supporter of that program and referred many other women as potential donors and volunteers. Even though she had a shelf life due to unfortunate changes in life status, she held her volunteering close to her heart because that volunteer manager took the time to develop her skills. Even when great volunteers have to leave for reasons beyond their control, we can take some comfort in the idea that we have turned an ally loose in the world. Just as you hear the adage that people may not remember our exact words, but remember how we made them feel, we can find solace in those who are with us a short time but will take away a positive feeling based on our treatment of them. I remember a volunteer who came to orientation and told me that she had spoken to one of the volunteers in the office briefly on the phone several years before. She told me that the volunteer was not only nice, but patient and kind. I can't say that the phone call was the only reason she decided to volunteer years later, but the fact that she remembered it tells me that if volunteers leave, they will be advocates for the mission because they were treated well and had a good experience.

Chapter 6

Can It Get More Complicated?

Could This Be Magical Thinking?

Once again, unless you work with volunteers, you have no idea what it is like. There is little chance that someone who does not deal with this vast pool of part-time, unpaid staff on a daily basis can possibly understand volunteer management. Hence, those who do not work closely with volunteers can engage in magical thinking. When you have little idea about something, you can operate under assumptions that are not true. If you were suddenly dropped into the middle of constructing an airplane, where would you start? Could you do it, or would you make serious mistakes that would keep the plane from ever being built? What we know little about, we cannot do well. Sometimes, knowing just a little about something is worse, especially if that bit of knowledge is incorrect. Those who do not work with volunteers cannot build our plane, and occasionally they have preconceived notions about how volunteers and volunteer services work. Thus, they operate from a point of view that may be unrealistic and a bit magical.

Magical thinking goes like this. The volunteer department has thirty-five or fifty or six hundred volunteers who are ready and waiting to be called. Surely, there is one who will drive a client to her daughter's home over three hundred miles away. There must be a volunteer sitting by the phone, happy to get dressed and run over to a community event on the other side of town because we forgot to request a volunteer the week before and now there is no representation for the organization. Surely, once volunteers have gone through orientation, they are committed to being helpful in any way they can. It's not that hard, is it? All you have to do is make a call.

Sometimes, it seems that requests for volunteers are akin to putting a quarter in the gumball machine. Put your quarter in, turn the knob and out rolls a gumball. You might get a blue one or a red one or a yellow one, but regardless of color, each one is perfectly round and tastes the same. There is comfort in the sameness. Volunteers are sometimes viewed like gumballs. Make a request, get a volunteer gumball. With gumballs, we know what we are getting. Gumballs are faceless. They have no personalities, no problems, and no quirks. They are all perfectly the same, operate the same, and serve the same. They are faceless helpers. Faceless numbers can do anything. Faceless numbers never give us any trouble and are always upbeat, sitting by their phones, eager to please. Faceless numbers are like the gumballs in the machine; you hold your hand under the flap and get your perfect volunteer. A faceless person always has the right temperament, personality, and skills for the job. Faceless numbers don't have any reason not to accept an assignment.

Our job is to weed through the gumballs, sorting them as we consider carefully who will be the best person for the task at hand and whether that person is available. If he/she is not, we defer to our second choice, then the third, fourth, and so on. Filling one task can take all afternoon as you call, leave messages, and speak to those who do call back, find out more information, and then call again, and again. Gumballs would just do what is asked without question.

When we look at our volunteers, we examine them closely, discerning their features, taking into consideration their personalities, talents, and skills. We then find the right person for the job. It takes a great deal of time and thought matching volunteers to tasks. If we have five volunteers available for a job, but all five are wrong for it, then we have to do some creative thinking before turning a person loose on an assignment, so we sometimes have to reach outside the scope of traditional volunteers.

We don't look at volunteers as gumballs. No, to us they are not even the proverbial box of chocolates. Volunteers are much more like that "everything" drawer in your house. In there you will find all sorts of interesting things: batteries, candles, screwdrivers, thumbtacks, markers, that broken pair of glasses you are eventually going to fix. The items in there are so varied, it takes rooting through the drawer to find the perfect tool for the job. Some items are broken, while some are purely decorative and others are quite useful. It takes time and effort and a great deal of looking to find the right tool. Unfortunately, not everyone who requests a volunteer realizes that. Thus, magical thinking implies that requesting a volunteer is as simple as buying a gumball. Because we know better, we need to educate those making the requests. Teach them about volunteers, about how volunteers want to help, are in it to help, but that they do not all share the same qualities, skills, and availabilities.

How many times have you been asked to supply a volunteer and wished that you knew more about the assignment? Do you find yourself asking volunteers to do a job and then have to make multiple calls about the particulars because the volunteer needs more information? Try and get as much information up front as possible.

Remind the person making the request that the more information you have, the quicker you will be able to get a volunteer and the better that volunteer will be suited to the job. If a volunteer needs computer skills, that is good to know. Details, such as there are five big dogs in a client's home, are crucial. There are always a volunteer or two that love animals and don't mind a house full of them. Knowing that the client and family smoke constantly will keep the embarrassing situation of a volunteer who is allergic to smoke having to leave the home after he/she gets there from happening. It also prevents the volunteer from having an aggravating experience. We all know that too many of those experiences turn even the best volunteers into a scarce commodity.

Magical thinking can also imply that when all else fails, get a volunteer. A hospice volunteer department was actually asked to have volunteers clean their inpatient unit. This plan would save that organization money, and what the heck—the volunteers won't mind. They certainly didn't become volunteers to have a meaningful experience. Another hospice wanted volunteers to stand by their chapel in shifts in case any family member went in. This way, family members would have a compassionate volunteer ready to greet them. Nice idea, but they did not take into consideration the many boring hours of wasted time the volunteer would spend waiting for that one family member to show up. After all, volunteers have nothing better to do, right? Besides, they're all retired.

A great many volunteer departments are asked to provide volunteers to honor staff. This is a tricky prospect, because some places successfully swap honors between staff and volunteers. Therein lies the key. If the staff regularly honors the volunteers, the volunteers will want to return the favor. However, if the volunteer department is putting on the luncheons, sending out the thank-you cards, hovering over the volunteers who are working, fetching coffee for that long project, then, no, the volunteers will not feel good about becoming hosts and hostesses for staff. It has to be a mutual admiration society, and all too often, the only people celebrating volunteers are those who are paid to do so. Volunteers notice the halfhearted speech at their banquet, the staff member who brushes by them every day, the team member who hands them an assignment and disappears without full instructions. They certainly notice where the thank-yous are coming from as well.

Volunteers come to us to do something worthwhile. Asking a volunteer who wants to make a profound difference in a life to simply clean or move boxes will not work if that volunteer feels as though that is all he/she is needed for. Occasionally, volunteers don't mind doing the mundane chores. They want to help. But if those chores become the way they are viewed, they will quit.

One volunteer told his volunteer manager that he was called by a team member and asked to sit with a client who was violent. Staff was cautioned not to go into that client's home alone. They were to visit in pairs, just in case. No one even thought to warn the volunteer department that the volunteer might be walking into an unsafe situation. Luckily, the volunteer manager was astute enough to speak to several staff members before placement. That way, he was able to intervene before something terrible happened. That is how magical thinking works. If there is a problem, the volunteer department might be able to solve it. Staff members deal with each other every day and rightfully look out for one another. They are witness to each other's strengths, gifts, and weaknesses. Since they don't know the volunteers as well, the volunteers become the faceless gumballs. No need to include Missy, we don't know her. No reason to warn Bob, we don't know if he is able to handle himself or not. Mixing staff with volunteers can lead to understanding and a sense of team. Mixers, parties, meetings, educational opportunities, and events are all good ways to put staff and volunteers together. Staff will then learn that the volunteers are real people with personalities, gifts, quirks, and heart. It is good for the staff to put faces to names and to learn about the volunteers. Staff will then not only look out for them, but will start to see them as team members and will even ask for specific volunteers for tasks.

Magical thinking also exists when staff expects a volunteer manager to implement any and every new idea. Sometimes, staff will look for innovative ways to help the organization. Without input from the volunteer department, they can formulate ideas or projects that may not work the way they expect. It is then up to the volunteer manager to point out the pitfalls along with the benefits of each project. The volunteer manager must be prepared to offer alternative ways or solutions. Negotiate with your superiors, always keeping in mind the big picture coupled with the interests and abilities of the volunteers.

A hospice wanted volunteers to help staff members at a large nursing home with activities for their residents. The hospice thought it would show good faith if their volunteers could help the overworked nursing home activities director dish out ice cream each Friday at an end-of-the-week party. The hospice administration presented the idea to the volunteer department staff, which gently pointed out the extensive training the volunteers went through so that they could visit with patients at end of life. The volunteers, when polled, unanimously said that they did not wish to serve ice cream at a nursing home to which they held no allegiance. They wanted to be with patients. Instead of abandoning the project, these creative volunteer managers came up with their own version of the plan, one which took into consideration the wishes of their volunteers. They came up with a group of volunteers who provided art and music for not only the hospice patients, but for the nursing home residents as well. The volunteers created a fantastic program, the nursing home was thrilled, and the hospice looked professional and helpful. It became a signature project, and the volunteer managers were able to expand it into other nursing homes with great success. At times, the best defense is offense, so be prepared to create working programs that will fill the needs of your organization while fitting in with your volunteers' goals.

Keep Your Change

Magical thinking also occurs when organizations do not see the effect sweeping changes can have on their volunteers. Jenny was a volunteer manager at an organization that cared for handicapped patients. There were two long-term volunteers, both of whom had been with the organization for many years before she became the volunteer coordinator. Jenny had started with the organization as a nurse and had had many interactions with these two volunteers during the course of caring for patients over the years. When Jenny accepted the job as the volunteer coordinator, she was particularly confident in her ability to fulfill patients' needs, since she had seen firsthand the many wonderful seasoned people who were volunteering.

Jenny quickly and comfortably slid into her new position. She built upon the existing volunteer force and soon had a well-run department. Then, several things happened at the same time. Management was replaced with new management. Competition started ramping up in the area and a large endowment was left to the organization. Changes followed at a rapid rate. Marketing became a more important aspect of the daily operation. The day-to-day patient care was analyzed and reformed, and new rules were introduced, many of them affecting the volunteers. Volunteers were asked to contact their churches and civic groups to see if a "planned giving" representative could come and speak about leaving estates to the organization.

It wasn't long after several of these major changes that Jenny heard from the two long-term volunteers, who called her and basically

said they were retiring. One said she had so many other commitments and had to give up something. The other said that her
children wanted her to spend more time with them. Instinctively,
Jenny knew that they both were trying to spare her feelings. They
were quitting because the changes were too much too quickly;
the atmosphere was not the same as it always had been. How did
Jenny know that? Many other volunteers left as well,some who had
been there a significant amount of time, and others who were new.
Those who stayed grumbled loudly about the new direction and the
lack of the warm, fuzzy feeling they had gotten when they joined.
Unlike employees, when the warm fuzzies are gone, the volunteers
may leave too.

Jenny's example is extreme, but it left her volunteer base riddled
with holes. She had to start over in many respects, so she ramped
up recruitment. The volunteers that stayed were reluctant to take on
new tasks and she described them as "waiting it out to see whether
they wanted to remain." It was a very tough, dark time for Jenny.
As much as she tried to explain and spin the changes as a positive,
the volunteers were not on board. They wanted the old organization back. Change is difficult for anyone. There is much written on
how to integrate change, but if the volunteers are not willing to
give change a chance, they will leave. Some may be there because
they like the status quo. Some may be so comfortable in their role
that at any hint of alteration they are gone. Employees for the most
part have to accept change. Volunteers technically do not. They
can walk away at any time without notice. Whether or not they
tell us the real reason is up to them. They do not have to give us
two weeks, because let's face it; they do not need us to be a refer-
ence for them if they seek out other volunteer opportunities. Our
organizations have to make change work for volunteers. We must
educate our organizations that change may be hard for volunteers
to digest, and giving them a forum in which the executive director

fields questions while explaining the reasons for change is helpful. Otherwise, volunteers will feel as if they are not worth the time it takes to include them in the new direction.

What a Toxic Waste

Sarah was a volunteer who worked in an inpatient unit at a large hospice. She arrived on the floor each week to sit with patients and read to them, and sometimes she would sing to them in her soft, gentle voice. She was a model volunteer, well liked by the staff and greatly appreciated by each family. For two years she joyously integrated into the fabric of the inpatient care unit. Then the unit director retired and a new director was appointed. Her management style was very different from the former director's and soon the staff became disgruntled. They could not hide their unhappiness, and morale became so bad that staff complained often and openly, even in front of the volunteers. In the midst of their discontent, they unwittingly drew Sarah and the other volunteers into the politics of their situation. Constantly irritated, they answered volunteer questions with snippy, exasperated replies.

Sarah quit. She gave a lame excuse about spending more time at her son's school, although she had recently told her volunteer manager that hospice volunteering was "my way of doing something for me." The volunteer manager pressed her for details, already assuming the real reason. Sarah finally admitted that the toxic atmosphere was ruining her volunteer time and causing her to think ill of the hospice staff. The volunteer manager could not assure Sarah that things would get better. In truth, things got worse and more volunteers quit. Sarah was offered another volunteer assignment in a different area of the organization, but she declined. Her experience was tarnished.

When staff members asked where Sarah had gone, the volunteer manager lied and said that she was taking a short break and would be back. Everyone missed her. The volunteer manager secretly hoped that Sarah would change her mind, but she never did. If the staff had been told the truth they would not have believed it, because they could not see the changes from any perspective but their own. When volunteers quit because of the actions of the agency or staff, it makes it extremely hard on the volunteer manager. Do you tell the truth? Do you just make excuses and hope the next volunteer isn't so sensitive? This is where magical thinking can take place. No matter what we subject the volunteers to, no matter how things are not what they have come to expect, no matter how badly they may get embroiled in the day-to-day operations of the organization, the volunteers should stick with us. Sadly, they won't. The majority of volunteers have every good intention. They want us to succeed and are willing to put up with some nonsense.

What they do not want is to become a staff member. They want to have the same consideration as a staff member, but they really do not want to hear about the poor management or the fact that raises are smaller or that there is no upward mobility. Volunteers want to have the wonderful experience we promised them during orientation. They view the staff as true angels, people who spend their days helping others. They know we are overworked. They know we are underpaid. They know we have it tough on most days. We don't have to remind them. What they want is to be associated with the people that taught them about the joys of volunteering, the ones who instilled inspiration and enthusiasm when they first arrived. Staff members can become very comfortable around volunteers, hence letting down their guard. We owe it to the volunteers to keep our complaints in the back room.

The Real Reason May Come Too Late

Madge was a volunteer who quickly became a favorite at her animal shelter. She helped the marketing department by sitting at fairs, calling donors, and recruiting other volunteers. One of the marketing staff members had a personal fight with another marketing staff member. They stopped speaking to one another except when absolutely necessary. The tension within the department was so thick that it became nearly impossible for Madge to function, let alone find any pleasure in her volunteering. It did not take long for Madge to quit. She informed the volunteer department that she was retiring due to extensive traveling coming up. She was going to see her children, take a cruise, and do some weekend jaunts. The volunteer manager took her reason at face value, as she had no evidence to the contrary. It wasn't until much later that another volunteer who knew Madge well told the manager the truth. By then it was too late. Madge had taken on another volunteer assignment with a different charity and was very happy. Could Madge have been salvaged? Perhaps, had the manager known the real reason, but we are not always going to know. We have to be very perceptive and constantly check on volunteers to be able to stave off an exodus caused by factors we cannot foresee. Our best and brightest volunteers may not be the ones we can manage less. They, too, need supervision and a constant watchful eye as we look for any unhealthy situations that may cause them to leave.

One volunteer manager spoke wearily of the magical thinking at her organization. She was orienting volunteers quarterly and actively recruiting them in between. Management started to pressure her, asking her to try to figure out a way to get more volunteers into the program. Unfortunately, a vocal member of management was told by a neighbor that it took too long to become a volunteer. That neighbor's words suddenly became the reality for all prospective volunteers and the volunteer manager was told not to let too much time elapse between a prospective volunteer's inquiry and his/her orientation. It was even suggested that the volunteer manager orient new volunteers one-on-one and not wait for scheduled orientations so that "no one need look elsewhere to volunteer." This attitude, the idea that when someone—anyone—expresses an interest in volunteering, we have to drop everything and accommodate his/her whims, schedules, and idiosyncrasies, is not realistic. Imagine if staff were hired in that manner. Let's take a look at how that scenario would play out. A person, let's call him Drew, would call and ask for the HR representative of the organization. Drew would say to the rep, "Hi, my name is Drew and I think I'd like to try and work as a case manager. I think that might be good for me." Drew would go on to say, "I am anxious to get started on this new career path as soon as possible. One of my neighbors works for your organization and said I should give you a call." The rep might say, "Well, Drew, let me take a look. We have scheduled a new employee orientation two months from now. Would you like me to reserve a spot for you?" Drew would sigh and say, "Gosh, I had hoped to be employed within the week. I really want to get started right away." If the HR representative operated under the magical thinking model, she would then tell Drew, "Well, Drew, I can see that you truly want to be here. We definitely admire your spirit. I'll tell you what. Please come in on Friday and I'll make sure we give you a quick one-on-one orientation to start." She would further tell Drew that there would be no need to check any of his credentials or his qualifications or references. She would come in on her day off to make sure that Drew had everything he needed. On-the-job training? Well, they would get to that at some point because, heck, it was more important to keep Drew from inquiring at another employer, wasn't it? It wouldn't matter that Drew had no formal training, or that he did not necessarily have the right temperament for the job, or that he had no intention of committing to the mission. It only mattered that he inquired, right?

Do the people we serve deserve well-trained, dedicated, vetted staff? Of course they do. Don't they also, then, deserve the same consideration when being helped by volunteers? If so, why are the precautions, stopgap measures, and controls pertaining to volunteers not given the same weight as those we have in place for staff? Once again, the volunteer manager—who wisely realizes that volunteers need to be committed, need to understand the importance of the work, and need to realize that the client is the focus—becomes the voice of reason. Volunteer managers who have experienced the work for a few years begin to see that those people who are in a tremendous hurry and will not wait for scheduled orientations are usually not the type of volunteer who is there to help. They usually have other motivations, and some of those motivations can overshadow the ability to do the work. Volunteering is not and should not be taken lightly. If our organizations do tremendous amounts of good work, then it should be a place where people vie to work and volunteer, not the opposite. A very wise volunteer manager from a charity in Africa once said that the charity viewed volunteers as the "cream of the crop." That charity, in the poorest of regions, demanded that volunteers fit within their rules. It was a privilege to volunteer there. Did they lack volunteers? On the contrary, they had many who were willing to jump through each and every hoop to be there. If we give the impression that we are desperate or spineless, then we get the volunteers we deserve. Our organizations have to be reminded that volunteers must realize that it is a privilege to do the work. The people we serve deserve only the best. Sure, we can take pride in numbers of volunteers, or we can take pride in offering the help of dedicated, caring individuals who are with us for the right reasons and are willing to fit into our framework, because ultimately it is not about the need to volunteer, it's about the volunteering.

Chapter 7

What Are the Right Reasons?

It is one thing to talk about the different circumstances that befall us as volunteer managers, to discuss and look at the ways in which our jobs can be alternately maddening and hilarious. Without a strong sense of purpose and humor it is not possible to sanely work under the many varied circumstances we find ourselves in on a day-to-day basis. Humor helps diffuse the stress and anxiety we might feel when things do not go smoothly. Humor is a release that keeps even the craziest occurrences in perspective, like the phone call from a volunteer telling us that she just made a blanket out of old newspapers to give to a client, or the staff member who wants the volunteers to put on a play he wrote. Humor grounds us, especially when we can share our stories with each other because we get the silliness without judging. The yang side of our sanity lies in the ability to clearly see the little moments that are not funny at all. They are the poignant, dear, touching moments that reinforce our decision to do this job. These moments have a way of dropping into our hectic days at the times we need them most. They drop in so quietly and unobtrusively that if we blink, we might miss them. There are four people standing in the office, the phone is ringing, assignments are piling up, and we just finished spending more time than we have with a volunteer whose daughter was diagnosed with Parkinson's disease. Most people would miss the moment, but not us, because we have trained ourselves to be in tune with the volunteers, families, and our clients. Even though two people are having a loud conversation right outside our door and our cell phone is now ringing because we haven't picked up the office phone, we can still feel the moment when it comes. We have learned how to detect even the slightest nuance in a volunteer's story, or the way his/her expression changes when he/she mentions the client's son who is a marine serving in harm's way. We intuitively hone in on a problem, and in the same vein sense the joyous moments, no matter how small.

You know the moment. A new volunteer, Tanya, fresh from orientation class, steps into your chaotic office one afternoon. It has been a hectic day. One of your most reliable volunteers was in a car accident. You have spent an hour on the phone with the volunteer. He is not hurt badly, but did break his leg and will have to be out for several weeks. He's such a stalwart that you have given him four assignments. He always gets the clients that are harder to place, because he treats everyone with professional respect and he has a healthy sense of boundaries. Now, you have to replace him with at least two other volunteers who are maxed out already. You have no idea who will take these four assignments, and you sit and mourn the lousy luck. That morning you were asked to get a couple of really good volunteers for a last-minute community fair that is coming up in two days. It's an important fair, well attended, and only the best representatives will do. A prospective volunteer is still hovering in your office. She would like to volunteer for your organization, but is not sure if she can do the job. You politely give her the dates of the next orientation and try to explain that you will help her ease into volunteering. She gets misty-eyed as she talks about her husband who was helped by the caring staff and volunteers two years before. You sense she would like to talk more, but she has been there for thirty minutes and you have so many calls to make. Just before she arrived, a staff member had poked his head in to ask if you would help unload some boxes from a donor's car. Knowing that the volunteer at the reception desk should not be lifting boxes, you went out and spent twenty minutes unloading the car, lifting out the worn items in her trunk she wants to donate and hugging her as she told you about her mother's illness. You have answered many calls that day, including two that were transferred to you because the person who received them heard the caller say, "I'm not sure who I should speak to."

If you are in a hospice setting, a patient volunteer called to find out whether or not his patient is allowed to go out of the nursing home in a wheelchair. The hospice nurse told him not to take the patient out of the facility, but the nursing home wants him to take the patient for a walk because it's a nice day. Since he needed an answer immediately, you had to track down the manager of that team, pose the question, and call the volunteer back. The volunteer then wanted to talk to you about substituting a different nursing home for the one is he currently visiting. It seems that he was already visiting his uncle in one on the other side of town and it would be more convenient for him to add his hospice visits to that nursing home trip. You told him, of course, although the nursing home he now wants to visit does not have as many patients as the one he is currently visiting. There is a volunteer in place at the one he wants to visit, leaving the one he is currently visiting without anyone. The apple cart is once again upset.

The prospective volunteer leaves with dates in hand. As she walks out the door, the new volunteer, Tanya, peeks into your office and tentatively asks if she is disturbing you. "I can see how busy you are. I can come back."

"No, no," you assure her, hoping she hasn't seen the deep stress that is framing your expression. "Please sit down," you tell her, reminding yourself that your mantra is to spend as much time as you can up front with each new volunteer so that he/she is confident enough to become a great volunteer. Thankfully, Tanya declines the offer. "I'm really on my way to the store," she says, "and I just wanted to stop by and let you know that I spent my first afternoon with Mrs. Black." Edna Black is the patient you carefully chose for this inexperienced volunteer. You thought they might get along well because when you observed Tanya in class, she seemed to have a quiet respect for older patients. She spoke in glowing terms about her dear grandmother. Mrs. Black has grandchildren in another state.

"So how did it go?" you ask, cringing at the thought that Tanya might not have done well. After all, you have enough fires to put out.

Tanya smiles. "I just wanted you to know how much I loved our visit. I feel like I've known her all my life. She showed me pictures of her children and grandchildren and told me about growing up in Tennessee."

You are starting to smile. Tanya's joy is infectious. "That's just great, Tanya. I knew you were a natural. I sensed that from the first time you walked into this office. Mrs. Black is a very fortunate lady."

Tanya blushes. She needs the praise to know she is on the right track. "I feel like we've known each other for years. I can't wait to go back next week."

Now you are smiling broadly. "I am so glad to hear that," you say. Glad is not the word. You are complete.

Tanya gets up to leave. "I just wanted you to know that," she says, as she walks out the door. She pokes her head back in for one last look, and says, "Oh! Thank you for teaching me how to be with her. It really is just like you taught us." She gives you a broad smile before disappearing. And you remember why you are here.

These moments are more precious than money, time, and routine. They define who we are and why we do what we do. There really is no other explanation for why we would endure the endless chaos and turmoil that make up our day-to-day jobs. We are not chaos junkies. We are not drama lovers. We are not prima donnas. We are driven by the deep sense that what we are doing is not only making a profound impact on our clients' lives, but that we are adding a spiritual gift to the lives of our volunteers. We are sharing with them the secret we do not wish to keep to ourselves. Helping others is a noble, fulfilling way to live.

Teaching volunteer orientation, conducting educational in-services, and mentoring new volunteers is good for your soul. Teaching orientation is the way to meet and get to know new volunteers. You can assess their weaknesses and strengths, which will help immensely when placing them in an assignment. Look at it as a resume in hands-on time. You also get to see your organization from a fresh perspective as the new volunteer introduces you to the way he/she views the work. It reminds you of the first day that you took on your role, and you remember your own nerves and anxieties as you entered the world of helping others. The longer you work for your organization, the further you are from those first tentative moments. It is good to be able to experience that nervous first again because it makes you all the more empathetic with the new volunteer.

By teaching and mentoring, you are forced to exude the enthusiasm necessary to attract and keep volunteers' interest. By telling anecdotal stories and giving examples of the mission, you are reinforcing it in your own eyes. Telling a group of volunteers who are looking to you to guide them about the profound effect volunteers have on your clients not only helps them, it helps you. It reminds you why you came to the job in the first place. You become your own cheerleader by virtue of cheerleading them.

You get to know the volunteers well by spending as much time up front with them as possible. You start to see them as your clients will see them. Who is a good listener? Who is the most empathetic? Who is funny, organized, sensitive, frightened? Only by spending ample time with each one will you know them before placement. Lastly, and this is a bit selfish, as you spend the time cultivating and mentoring them, you begin to feel a deep sense of accomplishment. You are guiding them on a journey that will impact and enhance their lives greatly. As you see them gain confidence and grow in ability, you can quietly sense that all is right in the world.

In hospice work, new volunteer orientation can last anywhere from nine to twenty-seven hours. It is a long time in a classroom, but is well worth it. For those of you who teach orientation for your volunteers, you know the feeling when the class is about to graduate and a few volunteers groan and say, "We wish this class was longer. We're going to miss it."

Miss it? Always, when a new class starts, you want to apologize for taking up so much time, for putting them through the rigors, for making them listen to you teaching them. But they are with you freely, and they have made the decision to sit and hear what you have to offer. Being proud of what you offer will not only make the new volunteers more confident in what they are about to learn, but will instill in them a sense that coming to class was the right decision in the first place. Don't apologize for making new volunteers go through training. New volunteers can hide their trepidation fairly well. Sometimes, they will tell you weeks later how frightened they were, how they were intimidated by the smiling seasoned volunteers whom they felt they would never live up to no matter how long they were with you. One of the more enlightening things a volunteer manager can do is to check with volunteers they've trained at pivotal points after the training. By surveying the new volunteers, we can learn what they have leaned, what they appreciated, what they feel was lacking, and what they would change. After they have gotten into the organization and volunteered for a time, they can better hearken back to training and determine what has actually helped them. Having a fellow volunteer survey them is even better, because they are normally more honest with a peer. And besides, if they have a complaint about you, they're not likely to express it to you, are they?

We've all heard the term *compassion fatigue*. When we are worn-out from caring for others, we experience a lack of sensitivity to anyone and anything. I happen to think that compassion fatigue is not quite what we experience in our jobs. Ours is more of a *passion fatigue*, because we have to be passionate about what we do and project that at all times. Every time a volunteer calls, comes into the office, inquires about volunteering, wants to recap an assignment, or needs to clarify what he/she is doing and why, we have to show the passion, not only for the work, but for them as well. Certainly, we show compassion for our clients, their families, our co-workers, and volunteers, but we have to do so with passion. It's almost as if we are starring in our own play, one that takes a great deal of enthusiasm and projection. Think *Oklahoma* and we are singing our hearts out, smiles on our faces. Day in and day out, that can be exhausting.

When employees are feeling unenthused about their jobs, they can grumble and complain in front of one another. That grumbling does not cause another employee to quit his/her job. In the volunteer world, if we complain in front of the volunteer who works by our side in our office, that volunteer will quit after a few times of listening to us whine. Therefore, we are forced to put on a "happy face" day after day.

Should the volunteer manager let his/her guard down, and allow the volunteer to see the stress, frustration, and weariness, then the mystique is gone. If we are brutally honest, the volunteers expect to see the same level of enthusiasm they saw during their courtship and orientation. They come out of training fired up and ready to go. If they enter the organization and find that the everyday work is dull, the staff is uninterested, and the volunteer department is continuously overwhelmed, the thrill will surely be gone. Nothing deflates and pops quicker than a balloon that was overinflated. Being careful not to paint an impossibly rosy picture can stop the false expectations from occurring during the initial training. We have to be honest with the volunteers, let them know that nothing is perfect, that our organizations deal with real people leading real lives, and that within that real world will lie the volunteering nuggets. They just have to have their eyes open to find them. We want them to be prepared for what awaits.

If we paint a glowing picture by only giving them anecdotal stories and examples of poignant moments, they will come to expect miracles every time they step into the world of volunteering. While it makes great theatre for volunteer orientation, too many stories of perfect successes will set them up for disappointment, and the specter of these great volunteers who go above and beyond will cause them to feel inadequate right out of the gate. On the flip side, stories about the hard parts of their jobs may be a great teaching moment, but too many of those examples will make the new folks think everything is way too hard. There is a delicate balance between the outstanding moments and the everyday moments that are truly outstanding in the lives of those we serve. Our choice of stories should inspire, encourage, teach, and assure the new volunteers that their work will be meaningful. How often have you heard a staff person say, "We couldn't do this without the volunteers!" The statement, although in many ways true, is a bit broad and meaningless. It would be better to tell a volunteer that the organization is able to provide more and better services to the clients because of volunteer help. There are many concrete examples that can be used, from statistics to anecdotes. You can tell the resale shop volunteer how much money was donated to the organization and exactly what that meant. Break it down into, "Fifty thousand dollars sent one hundred children to camp. And here is the story of one of those fortunate kids." Real stories and faces carry tremendous weight. It brings everything home.

When a volunteer wants to tell us a story about the experience he/she had, it is usually for a very good reason. These stories are where the nuggets lie; they are the stories we can share with our new volunteers. They are also the stories that should accompany our end-of-the-year reports. If we just had the time to check in with each volunteer every time he/she did something for us, we would have binders full of great stories, but unfortunately we don't have that time. However, when a volunteer makes a special trip or a phone call to tell you something, it usually is worth hearing.

There are also those volunteers who may not do the profound in-the-trenches work. They may come into the office, file a few papers, do a little data entry, or mail some letters. They wouldn't win any volunteer of the year awards, but they are indispensable because they are funny and kind and enjoyable to be around. At least those are the sort of volunteers we should surround ourselves with in our offices, because we need those personalities by us as we face our hectic days. You know the type, the ones who light up the room with their quick smiles and delicious jokes. They are the chocolate sundaes at the end of a day of bologna sandwiches. They may try to mother us or protect us, or may even try to fight our battles for us, but when it comes down to it, they really care not just about the mission, but about us personally. It happens after they have gotten to know us for a while, observed us under pressure, seen the way we treat volunteers, clients, and staff. They are privy to our very character and they like what they see. These are the volunteers that we can relax around, joke with, and let our guards down with. They want to help us succeed. When their shelf life is up due to illness, moving, or whatever circumstance ends their volunteering, we mourn. No one but we know the value of these volunteers, because we, like the clients who are served by great volunteers, benefit from their presence. It is a reminder of the joy that volunteers bring to their work. If we feel relief when we see our special volunteer, imagine how clients feel when they see their volunteer show up at their door. It is a good thing that we also receive the loving help from our volunteers, because it makes us appreciate and advocate for them all the more.

Having some special volunteers that you know as well as you know your dearest friends means that most of the volunteers do not fall into this category. If our special volunteers tell us why they are leaving, we know they are telling the truth because we have that kind of relationship with them. Other volunteers may not tell us their real motive, because for some reason they cannot or choose not to be honest with us. At times we will wonder. At times the circumstances will not make sense. Logistically, we cannot spend great chunks of time bonding with each and every volunteer. We have to find ways to make all volunteers feel comfortable, able to voice their feelings and opinions, and give each volunteer an open-door policy. Sometimes, having existing volunteers mentor other volunteers is a way to forge a connection. Trustworthy, seasoned volunteers can mentor the newcomers by simply checking in with them periodically, hearing their situations and reporting any potential problems that need attention. There are studies that show if an employee has a good friend at work, job satisfaction increases. Volunteers would like us to be their good friend. If you have too many volunteers to do that, then the next best thing might be several volunteers befriending all the newcomers. This can also be an excellent job for those volunteers who no longer can physically come to the office, but are willing to make calls from their home. That way, you've extended their shelf life as well.

Chapter 8

You Did What?

Not everyone who works with volunteers carries the job title of Volunteer Coordinator or Manager of Volunteer Services. For a huge number of those who manage volunteers, this job has been lumped in with all their other duties. There may not be enough volunteers to warrant a full-time position. The program may not be formalized. Volunteers may be an afterthought. For those volunteer managers, the challenge is deeper and part-time. When there is no formalized program that can mean no rules, no stopgap measures, no procedures, and no recourse. That type of volunteer management is chaos at best. If there are only two volunteers to manage, chaos can be channeled. However, volunteers are like potato chips. You can't just have one, so for these volunteer coordinators, management becomes learning by the seat of their pants.

Getting Into Real Trouble

I recently had a conversation with an activities director at a large nursing home. At any given time, between ten and fifteen volunteers were visiting the residents. During the summer months, she would welcome the local high school students who needed hours for graduation and would see her volunteers increase to twenty. As a busy activities director, her management of volunteers consisted of having them sign an agreement paper and then telling them to visit the residents and report to her if they had any problems. She was extremely busy and could not find the time to be a recruiter, mentor, human resources director, mediator, coach, and evaluator. With changing regulations and programs within her industry, she could barely keep up with her primary job.

Unfortunately, it never occurred to her to elevate one of her volunteers to a leadership position. She suffered from what can be called the "too busy to ask for help" syndrome. You have seen this. A department or person is swamped and overwhelmed. You keep offering volunteer help. They tell you that they would love it, but every time you offer a real live volunteer, they balk. They don't have or can't take the time to train someone to help. It's better for them to swirl in the tornado they know than to stop and take on a possible solution.

The activities director had a volunteer named Amy. She was the perfect volunteer for this part-time volunteer manager (PTVM) because she caused no headaches. She truly understood the nursing home atmosphere. She looked past the sometime smells, the vacant looks on some residents, and the overworked staff. She did not complain, but rather treated each resident as though he/she was part of her family. Amy checked in by spending no more than two minutes updating the PTVM. Amy was gold.

There was one particular patient, Carrie, a young woman who had suffered multiple strokes when she was just thirty-two years old. Carrie was difficult to understand, but Amy managed well and soon was spending most of her time with Carrie. They became very close, which on the surface is what volunteering is all about, isn't it? We encourage volunteers to bond with those we serve. We believe it is in the best interest of the client and the volunteer. While most volunteers have the strength and courage to handle this intense bonding, there are always going to be some who can't. The client might resemble a family member. There can be a deep need within the volunteer to be needed, so prolonged contact with a person who clearly needs him/her can trigger those feelings. These are the issues that don't come out during our initial interviews.

Amy became attached to Carrie. She began to bring her small presents. She spent most of her time with Carrie. She started to view herself as Carrie's "advocate" and began to formulate opinions on everything from her care to her family's involvement. The PTVM, because she was too busy and because Amy simply poked her head into the office and said hi, did not see the deepening bond that was becoming unhealthy.

One day Carrie told Amy that she wanted to live with her. Carrie haltingly told Amy that she loved her and that Amy was the only one who really made her happy. That day Amy went home and called a lawyer. She petitioned to become Carrie's legal guardian. The nursing home became embroiled in a legal and publicity nightmare.

Carrie's family was in an uproar. They removed Carrie from the nursing home. The activities director/part-time volunteer manager was blamed. Amy was not allowed back into the nursing facility. Eventually the legal tug-of-war ended, with Carrie's family winning. Amy was not heard from again at the nursing home. Not long after, the PTVM quit and took time off from working in nursing homes.

Sometimes, well-meaning volunteers get into trouble. Actually, it seems as if the well-meaning ones get into trouble more often than volunteers with ill intent. Usually, we spot the volunteers with ill intent right away and weed them out quickly before they can do any damage. If something seems off with them, we watch them like hawks. We're on top of them all the time, analyzing every move, waiting for the first inkling of wrongdoing so we can stop them in their tracks. It's the volunteers we trust, the ones who have wonderful attitudes and truly want to help, that can easily slide into the area of trouble. We don't watch them as closely. We don't question their judgment as often. We might not see the early warning signs most of the time. With these volunteers, we are blindsided. Volunteers all need our attention. It is everyone's job to pay attention to them. In Amy's case, she started to complain about Carrie's care, but the staff did not realize they should have said something to the PTVM. They thought they had no recourse. Had they kept this busy manager abreast of Amy's changing attitude, the disaster might have been prevented. We need to educate staff and tell them to let us know when a volunteer is acting out of character or has changed in any way. Many eyes and ears will keep tabs on even the best of volunteers.

You Are Not Serious, Are You?

A very long time ago I was talking to a volunteer coordinator at a hospice that had a faithful, long-term volunteer named Dottie. Dottie had three and four patients at a time and was driven to be the best volunteer this hospice had to offer. The coordinator attributed her zeal to the wonderful care given to Dottie's husband when he died on the program many years before. Because she was the best volunteer, Dottie was assigned to a family that truly needed a special touch. The patient was a young business owner, a loving husband and father of three whose illness caused a tremendous loss of income. The hospice helped with finances as much as it was able to and Dottie was called and apprised of the family's situation. She eagerly accepted the assignment.

One day, a staff member called the family to make appointments to see the patient. There was no answer at the house. The member called again later in the day. There was still no answer. The staff member asked the volunteer coordinator to call Dottie to see if she knew why the family was not answering their phone. There was no answer at Dottie's house, so one of the staff members drove out to the patient's house and found that the family was not there. As there was no widespread use of cell phones at that time, the staff member was alarmed. Equally worried, the volunteer coordinator called another volunteer who was a friend of the missing Dottie. The coordinator was told that Dottie had driven her patient and family to a mountain cabin for a quick vacation. Fortunately for everyone, Dottie and the family returned two days later, none the worse for wear. The family was actually very grateful for the free trip paid for by Dottie.

Dottie was reprimanded and made to promise not to be so irresponsible in the future. She became the stuff of lore at that hospice and her exploit was chuckled over since it did no real permanent damage. I often wonder what happed to Dottie and her volunteering. The coordinator said that Dottie agreed not to take patients on trips, but she did not seem to agree that it had been a bad idea in the first place. Fifteen or twenty years ago, volunteers at hospice were allowed to be involved in the patients' everyday affairs. The fact that Dottie was not fired immediately speaks more to the time than the organization.

Over time, the roles of the volunteers have shifted considerably and liability has shaped the way in which a volunteer can interact with our clients. Today, Dottie would have been dismissed without any fanfare. Years ago, the attitude was different, and frankly, volunteers were different as well. The world is changing rapidly around us, and volunteerism is reflecting those changes. The world of volunteering has morphed from an "anything goes" management style to tight rules, and regulations based on liability, risk management, publicity, competition for public funds, and scrutiny by an increasingly involved social media. As the new volunteers enter your organization, they are more inclined to understand these new trends. Our long-term volunteers may need a great deal of help getting on board with the changes.

You Could Have Knocked Me Over with a Feather

Michelle was a godsend. The organization she volunteered for had just embarked on a risky new mission and opened a thrift store, an undertaking that was years in the making and took a great deal of persuading for the board of directors to finally give the go-ahead. The volunteer department of this high-profile charity had worked tirelessly, promising revenue, community involvement, and valuable exposure. After the initial work, the store opened with a manager at the helm who had previous retail experience and a group of newly recruited volunteers. It was a small shop, a boutique-style gift store in a high-traffic area of a busy shopping center. Michelle came on board through another volunteer's recommendation, and the fact that she had owned and operated a clothing store for years made her invaluable. The volunteer department was very excited, because Michelle represented a new breed of volunteer, one they had never had success recruiting in the past, one who never would have volunteered to help clients or in the office or in fund-raising. She was an example of the department's expanding sphere of influence as the store quickly began attracting this new breed of volunteer.

The store opened to good reviews from the community. It was attractive and fun, and the organization saw an uptick in reaching the community with information about its programs. Michelle quickly became the go-to person for decisions on design, pricing, customer service, and recruitment of volunteers with a similar retail background. She gave excellent advice, showed the store manager how to get the most for each item, and helped the store begin to show a profit. As the manager relied more and more on Michelle, the other volunteers started to look upon her as an assistant manager, although there was no such title. But, she was directing the day-to-day operation when she was there, which was several times a week, and the store manager was relieved to have someone so knowledgeable as second in command. The organization's management team soon took notice, praising the store and the remarkable success it already had attained, not only from a revenue standpoint, but also in the increased funding from the surrounding community.

One day, however, a thrift store volunteer, Janice, was observed by another volunteer accepting a rare and valuable item from a donor. The store manager saw her take the item, price it, and then proceed to purchase it on the way out after her shift was over. The item was priced ridiculously below its resale value. When confronted, Janice said that all the volunteers did that, and were only following the example set by Michelle. Upon further investigation, it was discovered that Michelle was systematically purchasing valuable donated items to sell at her friend's antique store. The other volunteers had numerous items stashed behind boxes or on the back room shelves, to be retrieved later. All were purchased at scandalously low prices. Michelle volunteered with a good friend of hers, Pat, and the two of them priced each other's purchases and made sure that they were at the register when the other checked out. The store manager was shocked, blindsided by the unscrupulous behavior of the volunteers. She could not fathom how these seemingly caring women could cheat the organization out of its donated items. She was also shocked at how blind she had been when the evidence was in front of her all along. Her faith in her ability to manager volunteers and the store was shaken to the core.

Now, all the tremendous effort to make the store a success seemed a lie. She wondered how the community viewed the store and how deep the corruption ran. Hurt and saddened, the store manager had to ask for help in resolving the situation. When the store had opened, no policy had been put in place regarding volunteers' purchases. It was assumed that the volunteers would buy an occasional blouse or trinket. No one thought that volunteers would exploit the store as a means for personal gain. The established group of volunteers was so polluted by the haphazard rules and regulations that when new rules were finally instituted, most either quit or became disgruntled. It took nearly a year to sort out the negative atmosphere and create a new team of volunteers. The store manager was so traumatized by her experience that she eventually quit. She had to endure the endless questions from upper management, other staff members, and volunteers. Because she did not see what was going on behind her back, the mess Michelle instituted grew until it was no longer manageable. Sometimes, volunteers can be too good to be true. Sometimes, they can be the answer to our prayers, and as the things in front of us look ideal, we forget or choose not to see what is going on behind us. Assuming that every volunteer has the purest of intentions can be a mistake. It doesn't mean that we have to be suspicious and question everyone's motives, but we do have to keep our eyes open. One volunteer's actions can affect a group of volunteers, if they perceive that whatever the lead one does is acceptable. Setting rules up front only protects us in the long run. Unscrupulous people see a no-rules situation as a breeding ground for their agenda. Rules also show we have given great thought to those we are helping. Our clients deserve the best from us. Imagine the lost revenue those volunteers racked up. By not paying the fair price for items donated, they not only stole from the clients, who would have benefited greatly from the increased revenue, they stole from the donors, who did not expect their donations to be pocketed by staff or volunteers. The store manager was very fortunate that she found out about the situation in the shop, instead of someone in the community reporting it to her superiors—or worse, to the press. However, that might have prompted change sooner. At least she rectified the situation so that no more damage could be done. Michelle and Pat quit, of course, when handed the new rules regarding the purchasing of thrift store merchandise. They did not even acknowledge their bad behavior, but simply picked up their purses and left. The volunteer department learned a valuable lesson also. Even if a volunteer does not work directly with the client or with the staff, he/she should at least have a vested interest in furthering the mission of the organization. Without a desire to help, motives tend to be self-serving.

Where Are You?

One volunteer manager who worked for an organization that cared for critically ill children recalled a volunteer named Scott. He was a very interesting man and came to the organization many years ago when men were unheard of as volunteers helping ill children. He was a successful banker who retired early and was well off. According to Scott, he was a radical '60s baby boomer turned corporate executive who was going back to his '60s roots and looking to become more community- and service-oriented. The volunteer manager was thrilled. Scott had been studying massage therapy, healing touch, and mysticism, and wanted to bring these cutting-edge alternative therapies to sick children. There were not that many volunteers who had Scott's skill set at a time when alternative therapies were just coming to light for many health-care organizations. Scott agreed to give classes to other volunteers and to help the staff initiate and recruit other massage therapists. The volunteer department's status at the organization was elevated for having brought Scott on board.

At first, Scott was reliable and enthused, and spent many hours setting up the program. After several months, Scott informed the volunteer department that he was taking a trip and would be gone for two months. He had booked the trip of a lifetime, a two-month immersion in Brazilian life and culture. The department staff wished him well, asking for postcards and putting his program on autopilot until he returned. Scott never came back. After three months had gone by, a volunteer department employee called Scott's phone number and left messages. After four months, the department wrote him several letters. After five months an employee drove by his house to see if anyone still lived there. Through a friend of a volunteer who knew Scott, the staff heard that he had met a woman in Brazil and was now applying for a visa. The department was stunned. Not only did Scott disappear, he never gave them the courtesy of an explanation. They quietly closed his file and started searching for a volunteer to take over the massage therapy program. They were hurt because Scott did not feel the same about them as they felt about him. They were vulnerable because he left them without so much as an afterthought. Upper management could not understand why this volunteer, who enthusiastically created a potentially award-winning program, would just disappear. The unsaid implication was that the volunteer department did not do enough to hold on to him.

After a year had gone by, the volunteer department started to look at the experience with a healed attitude. Upon analysis, they realized that Scott could not have viewed the massage therapy program the way they did. Their excitement and enthusiasm was fueled by their organization's recognition of a wonderful pilot program and the discovery of a "professional grade" volunteer. Their entire working world revolved around recruiting and developing new volunteer talent, and Scott was akin to striking it rich. Scott, on the other hand, was just discovering his retirement, and their organization was just one stop on a long journey of self-discovery born out of his '60s sensibilities. Scott was out for adventure, as well as inner awareness, and the volunteer managers had to admit that all the signs for Scott's departure were there. He had told them that he wanted to set up the program, not manage it. He had told them that he had many "irons in the fire," and had made it clear to them that he loved traveling and adventure. In a painfully honest moment, they realized they had built Scott into something he was not. And then, in a healthy look back, they celebrated all the good they had reaped from Scott's short tenure with them. His several months' devotion gave them the basis for a terrific program, one that eventually was managed by staff and volunteers combined. When the volunteer department staff added up Scott's hours, they noted that he volunteered more hours in the months he was there than many volunteers had over the years. His shelf life was tied to the creation of a project or program, and once he felt that his goal had been accomplished, he was ready to move on. We can't expect volunteers to hold our hands at every turn, especially those volunteers we depend upon for greatness. At some point, they must and should turn the reins over to us.

When volunteers give what in their minds is all they have to give, we have to be able to let them go. We have to realize that volunteers may not have the same idea about volunteering that we do. When Scott saw that the program he initiated was ready to go, in his mind his work was finished. Scott was not interested at all in the day-to-day operations of the program, nor did the tweaking and fixing the glitches appeal to him. The day-to-day operations of the project were boring to this man who was ready to live his retirement to the fullest and had the financial means to do so. The children's charity was just a station on the adventure train. Instead of focusing on losing Scott, the volunteer department staff at this charity focused on what they had gained from him and they moved forward, which was not only good for their own well-being, it benefited their organization, because they eventually found a volunteer and a staff member to run the program.

We must stop looking at volunteers as all the same, with the same commitment, focus, and ability to give. Whereas many of our volunteers will be with us for a long time, a volunteer like Scott is more akin to a consultant than an employee. If you deem these types of volunteers as volunteer consultants, the implied message is they will not be with you for long. They will come in, consult, and move on to their next phase. Scott was this type of volunteer.

The notion that volunteers must be permanently attached to our organizations has to change with the changing volunteer roles and the changing ways in which volunteers view themselves. Baby boomers and those who follow them are going to be more interested in projects with real starts and finishes than their WWII generation counterparts. If we look around at the world of employees, we see that, unless economic reasons prohibit, people tend to move around. Perhaps we are all more inclined to look for better positions, better conditions, and more satisfaction elsewhere. Why would volunteers be any different? If filing, making phone calls, and visiting clients becomes less and less exciting, what do we think will happen? We can't make all circumstances perfect for every volunteer, so we do our best and hope that he/she finds the work as enriching as we do. Now, we do have ways to help them see the power of their volunteering. Holding meetings with inspirational speakers, sending thank-you cards, or getting quotes and testimonials from those whose lives have been touched are small and easy ways to help volunteers see the beauty of their work. Go with them on occasion. If they see your pride and satisfaction in their work, they are uplifted. Ask your superiors to send a note of thanks. Give the volunteers as many educational opportunities and ways to grow as you can. It fortifies them. Check in with them after an assignment. Showing that we are aware of their contribution goes a long way. But when you have set the groundwork for a volunteer to continue with your organization and he/she chooses not to, don't assume that it is always your fault. Motivations are as varied as volunteers, and unless every employee that works for your organization stays employed until he/she drops, you can assume that volunteers will be no different.

Chapter 9

Why Do Volunteers Have a Shelf Life?

I was visited by a volunteer named Kathy the other day. She had been a volunteer for more than twelve years and was always reliable and prompt, with a good sense of humor and a solid understanding of the mission. She is one of those volunteers you can feel good around because she's comfortable with who she is and with the chaos and bumps in the road. Checking in with her has always been a pleasure, and as she performs the same duty every week, she is an expert at her job while forging long-term relationships with the other volunteers.

Kathy came into the office, sat down, and exchanged the usual jokes and happy pleasantries. She then became serious and said, "I need to talk to you." She proceeded to address a list of small things that have been bothering her. The things that she listed were results of procedural changes within the organization, rules and procedures that were implemented due to outside regulations, trends, or an organizational desire to do things more efficiently. Trying to explain the reasoning for these changes fell on deaf ears. She apologized and then tendered her resignation.

I've seen it before, this same scenario playing out as a volunteer tries to explain why he/she was quitting. These volunteers probably spend a great deal of time and feel quite a bit of angst trying to come up with plausible reasons for leaving. These volunteers, the ones who have faithfully served, enjoyed their time, cherished the lessons learned, and will cherish the memories they have made, will work to find a plausible excuse for leaving. It may be some petty grievance, health reasons, changes in lifestyle, or the new rules and regulations. In truth, the real reason is obvious, although I've never encountered or heard of a volunteer who honestly said, "I'm just tired of it."

I asked Kathy if changing her day would help. She said no. I really didn't expect it would have made a difference, but one has to try. Kathy had reached her shelf life. She was done, having spent more time than most faithfully doing a job week after week. If you think of it, how many of us do the same thing in the same manner for twelve years? Not many of us could last that long. We had gotten much more from Kathy than we had any right to expect. Instead of feeling as though we had failed her, we need to be thankful for her many years of service. Before you take me to task, yes, I did offer her other jobs and other schedules. We left it at a three-month breather from volunteering, and after the three months we would revisit other options. That may be all she needs. Changing positions may work. I certainly hope so. She is a great volunteer and our organization is much richer with her helping. But if she decides not to continue, then that is all right too.

Employees regularly leave. We don't chase them down in their new positions. We wish them well. We try to create an atmosphere that will keep the good ones for a long time. As volunteer managers, we have the added challenge of keeping really good volunteers coming back year after year simply by us being good volunteer managers. We don't have raises to dole out; we just have the satisfaction of a job well done, camaraderie, socialization, learning, and other very worthwhile perks of volunteering to offer. We can't, however, stop the inevitable conclusion of a volunteer and his/her journey. It will end, whether by death or decision, and it behooves us to realize that we are not miracle workers, clamping onto volunteers because not to do so would result in some sort of self-imposed failure on our part. It is time we realize that volunteers journey with us for many diverse reasons and that there will be an eventual completion of their journey, one which is supposed to end at some point, one which we can embrace and be thankful for while they are with us. Volunteers are as varied as any other group. To think that every one of them comes to us for noble, selfless reasons and will stay as long as the work is worthwhile is ignoring the complexities of the individuals we encounter. The work is worthwhile, always. It is the nuance of each and every volunteer's perception and motivation that alters the outcome, not the work itself.

Granted, some experiences are doomed from the beginning, and sometimes our organizations or we are at fault for that. When that happens, yes, we need to mourn and learn so that really good volunteers are not failed in the future. That is what we can beat ourselves up for, not for every single volunteer whose time has come and gone. Do we make mistakes, fail to do right by some volunteers? Absolutely. But do we need to blame ourselves for each and every volunteer that leaves due to circumstances beyond our control?

It Was All Good Until...

Kurt was a once-in-a-lifetime volunteer I heard about several years ago. He was a gifted artist, a celebrity of sorts in his hometown and a man very generous with his talents. A local charity that serviced disadvantaged youth began an art therapy program and Kurt, when he heard about the charity's need for volunteers, offered his services.

He helped the charity establish a way to engage their youthful clients in creating meaningful art projects that were not only beautiful examples of their developing skills; they were therapeutic tools in assessing life choices. Kurt spread the word among his sizeable group of artist friends and soon the charity had a thriving program.

One day, the volunteer manager was asked to contact Kurt, to see if he could help a young man who wasn't a client but truly needed a helping hand. She explained that this young man was referred by his teacher because he was having social anxiety and could not relate to his peers. Kurt agreed to help the young man. After several weeks of patiently instructing the young man at his home, Kurt felt as if he had accomplished his objective. The young man produced two paintings that were moody and hauntingly beautiful. He seemed to thrive on the special help and the charity was very grateful.

Kurt was puzzled as to why the young man lived in a very expensive part of town, but he trusted that the charity had referred him for good reason. The young man did seem like he needed some personal attention and responded well to the art lessons. Kurt resumed his work with the disadvantaged youth.

A few months later, Kurt read in the newspaper that a sizeable donation had been made to the charity he was volunteering for. With interest he read the name of the donor and realized that he was the father of the young man Kurt mentored some months before. Curious, Kurt wondered if his involvement had anything to do with the donation. He even hoped that the father was so impressed with the program that he decided to donate money to further the great work.

Buoyed by that thought, the next time Kurt was in the charity's office, he sought out the donation officer, who was out that day. His secretary was available and only too ready to gush over the size-able donation, claiming that the charity had been "trying to hook that guy for a long time." Kurt was enraged. He tracked down the volunteer manager and demanded an explanation. The volunteer manager, who had only done what was asked of her, was flabbergasted. She had no answer for Kurt but promised to look into the matter.

Shaken, she spoke to the donation officer, who told her not to worry, that really the donor just needed proof that their program was worth the money the charity was seeking from him. Horrified, the volunteer manager asked the donation officer to call Kurt. He never did. Kurt not only quit, he took more than half the remaining artists with him, and was extremely vocal about his poor volunteer experience when speaking to other artists who could have been potential volunteers. The damage inflicted on the program was insurmountable and eventually it fizzled. The volunteer manager could not keep enough artists to continue the work. She mourned over all the youth that would never benefit from the mentorship. Disheartened, she eventually left the profession and found a job in retail.

We know our volunteers are not stupid, especially accomplished volunteers such as Kurt. He was already a tremendous asset to that charity, not only in clients served, but in publicity, goodwill, and references. He elevated that charity to new heights. When our organizations try to deceive volunteers or use them as pawns in marketing and publicity, it backfires. Not only does the offended volunteer quit, he/she spreads the word about the deceitful organization. Volunteers can become enraged over an assignment that they perceive as suspect or for the wrong reasons. They sign up for specific activities and are not willing to become objects for any staff member to use. We need to stand up for our volunteers at all times. If we suspect that a staff member is using a volunteer as a marketing tool or donation bait, we have an obligation to demand an explanation. We also owe it to the volunteer to tell him/her the truth. But if, for some reason, you are not able to block a deceitful use of one of your volunteers, when that volunteer complains or quits, you should interview him/her and document the reason he/she left. Too often, volunteer managers protect the offending staff member from scrutiny when he/she causes a volunteer to quit. If we do not approach the problem with a professional desire to stop the offending behavior, then we will lose more volunteers.

When documenting an exit interview with a volunteer who feels he/she has been treated improperly, be sure to include quotes. Avoid subjective reporting; stick strictly to the facts by recording, "I was so mad when I found out that I was being used to procure a donation. That is beyond underhanded."

Thar She Goes

Cindy was a volunteer at a large nursing home. Her husband had actually been a resident of the nursing home for many years and had recently died. Cindy was grateful for the love and care the staff had shown her husband of forty-three years, Will, so she opted to volunteer a month after his memorial service. The activities director, who was a part-time volunteer manager, was apprehensive about having Cindy as a volunteer, because she knew Cindy had not had the time to properly grieve. But she also knew Cindy was a kind and caring wife and a lovely human being. Besides, she really needed volunteers. Cindy threw herself into her volunteering, visiting many lonely residents and caring especially for the elderly gentlemen that she happened to visit. Cindy seemed driven to keep the male residents happy and content, tending to them as she had to her own husband. The activities director kept an eye on Cindy, astutely recognizing that she was utilizing her volunteering to process her grief. As long as Cindy seemed all right, this part-time volunteer manager reasoned, there would be no problem.

After six months, the nursing home was sold to a national corporation and administration changed overnight. The new administrator took the nursing home in a new direction and changed many rules and operations. The change was hard on the seasoned staff, and they complained. Many sought jobs at other area nursing homes. A new, younger, and less experienced staff was hired.

Cindy got lost in the shuffle. The activities director stayed, but acquired new duties and could not spend much time with the volunteers. Cindy began to complain about the way things were now run and how the staff wasn't attentive to the residents. She made the comment that she was almost glad her husband Will was not alive to see the way the nursing home had changed.

When the complaint came in, the activities director was at first surprised and then resigned. Cindy had observed a new aide treating an elderly male resident gruffly. Cindy blew, shrieking at the aide that she was an "uncaring young bully." Her ranting was heard down the hallways, causing the visitors to be alarmed. Without any fanfare, Cindy dropped her badge onto the activities director's desk and left, her anger and sadness splayed across her face.

Herein lies a challenge we face at times. We suspect that a volunteer has the potential to do something wrong, or we feel that a volunteer is getting frustrated and cannot handle the sometimes rapid changes within our organizations. Volunteers are not part of the organization's discussions about how to handle day-to-day operational situations because they are not part of upper management. Rarely does a volunteer manager sit at the pinnacle of management in an organization, so decisions regarding company policy and volunteer involvement are frequently made without the very stakeholders who are affected by policies. Volunteers receive their information through their volunteer manager. We can inform, cajole, lead, and hold volunteers' hands, and yet independent of us, they may make a decision to do something unacceptable. Sometimes that decision is a blowup, as in Cindy's case. Would she have continued volunteering and working through her grief without incident, had the nursing home remained unchanged? Perhaps. But rarely do things stay freeze-framed in time. Things do change, and often.

Our volunteers have to be able to weather changes. They may not come to our meetings. We may not get the time to properly inform them of new policy before their next volunteer outing. They may not like the new tenor or the new rules or direction, but they have to be able to adapt and we must help them. However, there will occasionally be that volunteer who cannot, under any circumstances, accept change. If we take into account that everyone has a right to his/her own actions and opinions, we can stop blaming ourselves because our attempt to help that one volunteer fell on deaf ears. When an employee is given new rules and regulations, do we automatically assume that he/she will never break them, nor do anything to embarrass or impugn the organization? It is foolhardy for us to think that by our sheer will and dedication, we will keep all volunteers from ever making a mistake. Look at your numbers and you will be amazed at the miniscule percent of volunteers who create problems for your organization. I would challenge any workforce to compete with those numbers.

Where the Loyalty Lies

Julius was a very reluctant volunteer, I was told by a volunteer manager that worked at a charity serving a large retirement population. He was recruited by this charity because he represented a point of view they felt might benefit some of their clients. This charity was starting a program that paired male volunteers with male clients who had similar career paths. In that service area, there were many retirees from a particular auto plant in the Midwest. This volunteer department thought it would be helpful to have fellow retirees from that plant deliver meals to clients who would benefit from the sharing of experiences from their working days. Julius was the president of a retiree group that consisted solely of these auto workers, so he was the likely choice for the pairing of his group with this charity's clients. At first, Julius was unsure about delivering meals, and did not think his fellow retirees would want to do an activity that was obviously "depressing." Although the department kept trying to convince him of the need, Julius was not interested until one of their group members became infirmed and made use of the meal delivery service. After the death of that fellow group member, Julius changed his mind and got involved. He recruited several members of his group and a volunteer orientation was conveniently set up the club's meeting place. Slowly, the group formed their own volunteer activities. When a retiree came onto the program, Julius would dispatch two of the trained members to that client's residence. The men would sit and interview the patient and family to assess their needs, and then assign two or three of the group members to visit and deliver meals once or twice a week. The charity was pleased at the creative use of volunteers and praised the department for thinking outside the box.

One afternoon, a social worker came into the volunteer office and sat down. The look on his face was enough for the volunteer manager to expect the worst. The social worker said that he had been at the residence of one of the clients who had been receiving visits from the auto workers group. He said that he observed a family member handing a check to Julius, who had just delivered a meal. When the social worker later cornered Julius and inquired about the check, Julius explained that families were often so impressed by his club and their visits that they frequently offered donations to keep the club afloat.

The social worker apologized to the volunteer manager for having to break this news, but insisted that the issue be addressed immediately. The volunteer department called a meeting that included Julius, the volunteer department, and the psychosocial manager. Although the volunteer managers explained to Julius that solicitation or acceptance of money from families was strictly prohibited, it fell on deaf ears. Julius countered that his group was providing the visits and that they should be able to take the money offered. After all, he reasoned, the families wanted them to have it. There was no way of knowing how much money had been collected or how many families had contributed because Julius was not forthcoming. Upon further questioning, Julius admitted that the members of his club freely talked about their need for funds to further the other charity projects they were involved with. The volunteer department was devastated. They never thought the retiree club had any intent other than providing fellowship and meals to homebound seniors. Sadly, the trust was gone, and in good faith, the volunteer department could not allow this group access to their clients any longer. Unfortunately, the department felt that all the work convincing the club to deliver the meals and the subsequent time spent constructing the project had been wasted. They abandoned the idea of recruiting any other groups.

This department was not able to see what a wonderful idea they had attempted. They only saw the collapse of the project. Sometimes, volunteers do not see the mission in the way we do. Maybe their buy-in is weak. Occasionally, volunteers take on assignments with minimal passion. Does that mean that those volunteers will always do a substandard job? No, they too can come to care about the clients we serve and the mission we offer. The good news is they probably will not get overly involved.

What the passion-challenged volunteer lacks in embracing the mission is made up for in lower instances of over-volunteering, calling and chatting with us endlessly, and general neediness. They come and go, content with minimal input and minimal interest in attending educational in-services, while keeping their own best interests at heart. With these volunteers, we have to make sure their own best interests do not create unethical behavior, such as selling products to clients or soliciting money from them.

Julius never fully bought into the mission, and by engaging his club he divided his already thin passion in two. Actually, he more likely divided his passion into a 90/10 cut, with 90 percent going to his club. By using him for only those clients who fit into his interests, this charity guaranteed that his interest would win. After all, Julius was the president of his club, which is a pretty good indication that he had a vested interest in the club's success. He saw the meal delivery as fitting into his club, not vice versa. By placing his club members with clients who had the same exact background, the visits became about the auto plant and not about delivering meals to homebound seniors.

Groups that volunteer may understandably align themselves with their own members and mission over your mission and needs. They may wish to reach out to you as a group, and by doing so gain something like strengthening their bond, attaining favorable press, or learning new skills. If we understand this form of group think, we can successfully incorporate groups in our volunteer programs. We should not expect every volunteer—especially those who belong to their own groups, organizations, or clubs—to elevate our mission above theirs. If we recognize the unique motivations of groups, we can create circumstances that will benefit both our mission and theirs as well. We can create a symbiotic relationship that may span many years of partnership between us and outside entities that are willing to give us a look.

Chapter 10

So Where Do We Go from Here?

Does it all boil down to motivations, circumstances, or just plain luck? Or is a combination of all the above what determines whether or not we can retain a group of productive volunteers? Is there really some magical formula that will give us the edge when it comes to finding and keeping volunteers? Can we look for a "one size fits all" approach? Hearing and experiencing all the various volunteer stories, it has become apparent that volunteer management is not a one-dimensional proposition. It is much more complex. There are certain tenets that hold true, like treating our volunteers with respect, giving them meaningful experiences, and expecting them to work within our rules and framework. In order to naturally retain volunteers, there are five points to remember.

Be Prepared for Volunteers to Leave

Circumstances play a larger role than we might think. As circumstances change for our volunteers, their perspective may alter drastically until their volunteering no longer fits within their overall plan. Keeping volunteers who would rather be somewhere else cannot last for long. Once they are no longer in it for their reasons, but are just simply hanging on, the light and spark that made them great volunteers goes out. It will only be a short time before they are gone. We cannot control the outside factors facing our volunteers. Life change affects us all. For the working person, giving up a paying job may be an impossibility. Giving up a paycheck is not something we can take lightly. Volunteering, on the other hand, does not involve financial hardship. If something happens to a volunteer, he/she may leave without even letting us know. You don't have to give two weeks' notice to stop volunteering. Remember, volunteers are normally not with us for forty hours. Their buy-in consists of a fraction of their week. During the other substantial hours, they are volunteering for other organizations, taking care of their families, working, playing, cultivating hobbies, traveling, and engaging in all sorts of activities that do not include us. For those of us who work with volunteers, change, nuance, intuition, and surprise are daily parts of our work. Each volunteer brings his/her own skills, personality, and unique value. They also bring their own set of challenges based on personality, life, and motivation. It is like shaking the kaleidoscope and seeing the pattern change with each look. Volunteers are not employees, although they are looked upon as unpaid workers. And when a volunteer leaves, try to look for the reason without assigning blame.

Set Yourself Up to Avoid Incidents

One of the things that drives volunteers to leave is lack of leadership. Unclear directions, poorly defined roles, and the sense that no one knows what he/she is doing will cause good volunteers to look elsewhere. Do not be afraid to expect excellence from your volunteers. Having rules, regulations, defined roles, boundaries, and in-services to reinforce your mission and the requirements for all volunteers are savvy ways to show that you are serious about helping your clients. Some volunteer managers erroneously think they have to let volunteers do whatever they want. After all, they are donating their time, aren't they? Look at it this way. If your organization accepts donations, does that mean it will accept a donation of rotted meat? There is a limit to what is acceptable, and anyone who offers his/her time does not have the right to change the rules you have set forth. Your first obligation is to your clients, and by stressing this to your volunteers, they will not only appreciate your commitment to those you serve, but will come to have this mantra ingrained in their volunteer psyche. Do not be afraid to enforce the rules, even with the best of volunteers. Without this control, you may find that you have anarchy.

Understand Volunteer Motivations

Motivations are as varied as the volunteers who come to us. Sometimes, the motivations are straightforward, such as, "I want to give back, because you helped me," or, "I really just want to help people." On the surface, these seem to be the best reasons for getting involved, for they are the altruistic, selfless reasons. But then, is there truly any completely selfless motivation? We must be prepared for the deeper and sometimes hidden reasons for volunteering. Our volunteers may not even realize that they have unspoken motivations. If people do not acknowledge their need to be helpful or their desire to be liked, then they might tell us they are simply looking to be of service. It is up to us to find that other reason so that we can keep them from losing focus. If their motivations are getting a job or filling time, we can't just dismiss them. They may eventually turn out to be great volunteers, given the time and encouragement. Therefore, it begs the question: are up-front interviews enough to tell us all we need to know about a prospective volunteer? The volunteer that interviews well may be the headache down the road and the hesitant, nervous one may just turn out to be one of the best volunteers you have. Giving volunteers a chance is a tough proposition, but do we really trust our first instincts exclusively? Some volunteer managers say they can size up a person on first contact and can tell whether or not he/she will be a good volunteer. If they can, more power to them, but there are people who have surprised the rest of us, those we didn't expect much from initially who pleasantly proved us wrong.

Orientation is one of the best ways in which to create a sense of attachment to the mission. There are many organizations that are smart in requiring volunteers to go through more than an informational session. Fully developed orientations prepare volunteers for situations they might face. They also give the new volunteers a chance to bond with other newcomers. The enthusiasm new volunteers feel is due largely to all the up-front time the organization has spent with them, especially if many disciplines are involved. The more we nurture them in the beginning, the more their fears are allayed, their questions answered, and their feeling of inclusion increases. By spending time with us and other staff and volunteers during orientation, they are drawn in by the speakers we choose and become assimilated into our framework.

It would be great if we could just ask each and every new volunteer, "So, how long do you plan on being here?" The truth is, they probably don't know themselves, but in their new enthusiasm, they no doubt feel like they will be with you for quite a while. One question we can ask them is, "Where do you see yourself in a year or two?" Although they might not really know, their answers can give us some insight into their overall thinking. The answer, "I plan on moving up in volunteer jobs, learning and growing as I go," is different from, "I hope to help get pet therapy going." Is the new volunteer project-oriented or journey-oriented? Do fresh volunteers have one specific job in mind, or do they like challenge and variety? Does the new volunteer value education or is he/she motivated socially?

What exactly does a volunteer need from us? One manager told the story of a new volunteer, Hazel, who was quiet but enthused as she left volunteer orientation at a large hospital. She was ready to roll up her sleeves and get to work helping the patients she was taught would benefit from her presence. She got started and immediately became attached to an elderly female patient named Minnie. Hazel promised Minnie's daughter that she would be with Minnie whenever Minnie needed her. Hazel began spending many hours at the hospital, as Minnie's daughter worked. When another hospital volunteer began her shift, Hazel refused to leave Minnie's room. The staff had to cajole and coax her out of the room. The volunteer manager called Hazel in to have a talk about boundaries. After chatting for a while, Hazel revealed that her mother had had surgery in a hospital in another state and died two years before. Hazel had not been at her mother's side and her mother died alone, unexpectedly. Hazel needed to assuage her guilt by keeping other patients from that same fate. Whether or not she was aware of it, Hazel was volunteering for the hospital for her own emotional needs. Many volunteers do that, most subconsciously, and it becomes the degree of the emotional or spiritual issue that dictates whether or not problems will arise. Volunteers who challenge themselves can be great volunteers. Others who have to fix themselves may fail when their focus is not on the client served, but on their own issues.

Treat This as a Profession

It is nice that people view us as kind and helpful souls. We do, however, owe our organizations, our clients, our volunteers, and each other a professional view of volunteer services. We must elevate our jobs to a profession and demand respect for the complicated work we do. The continual education of not only fellow staff and administration, but the general public as well, will go a long way to establishing volunteer managers as professionals who provide a great service to our communities. We must look professional, act professional, and manage in a professional manner. By sweeping the difficulties we face under the rug, we foster the notion that our jobs are easy or silly or not worthy of respect. By continually showing the value of volunteers, we make the case for the wisdom of having great volunteer managers.

Standing up for volunteers and the work they do is not pushy or aggressive. In meetings, bring up the contribution volunteers made to the project being discussed. When hearing about future plans, chime in about the ways volunteers can help. Prepare reports that show not only budgetary value, but the human side to volunteer contributions. Advocate for the fair treatment of volunteers and intervene when you feel they are not being treated with respect. You are their manager, and you are the one who can make your organization see their worth.

Try to Retain Good Volunteers

The good news is most volunteers have wonderful intentions, are ready to fit within the scope of the mission, and become fantastic spokespersons for our organizations. Daily they are out in the community, talking, recruiting, and directing clients, donors, and other volunteers to us. If a great volunteer brings in a prospective volunteer, chances are that person will be at the very least a good volunteer, since he/she has been vetted by someone with proven good instincts. If a mediocre or marginal volunteer brings in someone he/she thinks would be good, we might have to take extra care when accepting him/her. I remember one volunteer who tended to be negative at times bringing one of her really good friends into an orientation. This new volunteer turned out to be really negative. That the two ladies were good friends was not a surprise. We gave the new volunteer a chance, but her negativity caused us to counsel her often. She eventually left and the original volunteer stayed, but her negativity improved, having witnessed her friend's departure.

If you look at your volunteer hours on a regular basis, that should tell you quite a bit. Check your hours against the list of volunteers who came into your program a year ago, two years ago, and three. Calculate your retention rate. See who is doing regular hours and look for reasons. Is it simply because each volunteer is an individual? Is it because the ones who give regular hours came from the same orientation? Were they recruited in a particular way? Does the staff they work with treat them like gold? It may give you some tips for the future.

Socialization can be a possible reason for volunteers to stay. Those volunteers that work in groups and form close relationships with each other may stay for two reasons, the mission and the camaraderie. Two reasons to show up may be better than one. Sharing the volunteer experience is crucial, which is why meetings are so important. At times, we, the volunteer manager, become the volunteer's best friend on the job. Although that may help the volunteer, it puts an undue burden on us. By having seasoned volunteers mentor the newer volunteers, you can create the buddy system, which is more than showing the new volunteer how to do his/her job. Let the seasoned volunteer take several new volunteers under his/her wing and be responsible for checking in with them regularly to field complaints and concerns.

This doesn't mean that the volunteer who is independent and prefers to work alone will quit before the ones who work as part of a group. The solitary volunteers may have a different "second" reason to keep volunteering. They may like getting out of the house, or appreciate the quiet time solitary volunteering affords. If we ask the successful, long-term volunteers who work independently what about their volunteering they love, we will find clues as to which new volunteers will be successful at that same job.

Luck sometimes brings us the best volunteers. We may be in line waiting to check out when we strike up a conversation with the person behind us, who ends up coming in to volunteer. We talk with someone who happens to know someone who has the exact skill set we are searching for at the time. We answer the phone to find that the caller really wanted to speak to another department, but becomes intrigued by volunteering after speaking to us. We've all had those bright spots that just defy any recruitment strategy. These moments make you wonder how many more people are out there who would make great volunteers and how do we reach them.

There are multitudes of recruiting strategies, but it boils down to finding the right person at his/her right time. So we ask, and ask again. If someone says no today, that does not mean he/she will say no tomorrow. As much as possible, spending time with potential volunteers draws them into the mission and gives them the courage to take the step. Most volunteer managers are too busy to spend one-on-one time with every person they encounter. Ask one of your volunteers to be responsible for spending one-on-one time with prospective volunteers. Often, volunteer managers are the last to utilize volunteers to help with their own work, preferring to give all the good volunteers to everyone else.

When we put a great deal of effort into volunteers by spending time with them initially, putting them through orientation, mentoring them, and following up with them, we certainly do not want them to leave. We should try and keep volunteers as long as possible, by offering them varied jobs, giving them time off when needed, and creating an atmosphere in which they feel productive and necessary. No one wants a revolving door of volunteers who come and go quickly. We all need folks to commit. A strong draw will keep volunteers coming back, and when they suffer from hardships and change, we can be there to walk with them. Most volunteers feel a sense of attachment and will stick with us for as long as they are able.

When they do leave, however, do not feel the crushing sense of failure. Logically look for the reasons they are no longer with you and learn from any mistakes made. Don't allow feelings of personal failure to overcome all you accomplished in creating an excellent volunteer experience. By being prepared, setting requirements, acting professionally, and understanding motivations, your volunteers will have a longer shelf life than you might have expected.

Made in the USA
Monee, IL
07 July 2020